MW01633824

The Leadership Runway

ENDORSEMENTS

How do Christian organizations grow beyond their founding leader? Steve Murrell has written a highly accessible, well-researched book on this critical subject. *The Leadership Runway* emerges out of biblical principles and is informed by decades of firsthand experience. I highly recommend it.

GREGG OKESSON, Ph.D.
Provost and Senior Vice President of Academic Affairs
Asbury Theological Seminary
Wilmore, Kentucky, USA

As always, Pastor Steve's books mirror his life's distinctions: clarity, wisdom, and courage. *The Leadership Runway* is an absolute gift for leaders who exist to honor God and seek the interests of others above self. He shares three non-negotiables in successful leadership transition: preparing emerging leaders, preparing the organization to be led by emerging leaders, and ensuring that experienced leaders finish well. Thank you Pastor Steve for being an exceptional leader to our Every Nation world!

RACHEL ONG
CEO, ROHEI Corporation
Member of Parliament, Singapore

Having been an emerging leader, I know how important and challenging successful ministry transitions can be. The Rev. Dr. Steve Murrell combines experience, education, spiritual maturity, and passion in *The Leadership Runway* with the hope of helping to facilitate godly transitions. Using real-world practical language, he helps readers avoid common pitfalls. Readers will benefit from Steve's pastoral heart and vulnerable posture. For the sake of our ministries and churches, I encourage ministry leaders to read and share this book.

THE REV. DR. CRAIG STEPHANS
Rector of Christ Church Anglican
Savannah, Georgia, USA

Why do some churches and ministries grow stronger and larger once their founders are no longer leading, while others do not? This insightful, Scripture-rich, engaging read identifies seven essential, doable preparation points necessary for the experienced leader to finish well. Steve Murrell writes with strong credibility: he and his wife Deborah have transitioned the senior leadership of a church or ministry to other leaders six times over the past three decades. Don't miss this book's opportunity to strengthen your capacity to finish well!

WARREN BIRD, Ph.D.
Co-author of 35 books including *Next: Pastoral
Succession that Works*
New York, USA

Dr. Murrell focuses on an obvious, but often ignored, truth: "nobody leads forever." You will discover *The Leadership Runway* is a gift for your present and future ministry. This gift includes relevant strategy, organizational leadership wisdom, and global experience. What fuels Steve's writing is an unmatchable passion for ministry to flourish beyond its founding leader.

ELLEN L. MARMON, Ph.D.
Director, Doctor of Ministry Program
Asbury Theological Seminary
Wilmore, Kentucky, USA

"No one leads forever." What a sobering thought! There is an important leadership conversation that is needed across the church worldwide, right now. This is especially important as the baby boomer generation ages and new, younger leaders emerge. I'm grateful that my friend Steve Murrell has courageously—and with raw honesty—tackled the subject of leadership transitions, turning his academic studies into a pragmatic guide to navigate a path that we will all one day tread.

WAYNE ALCORN
Senior Pastor, Hope Centre
Brisbane, Australia

I can't think of a better leader to help us think about one of the most challenging aspects in making great transitions. Steve Murrell is leading a worldwide ministry that impacts nations by continually raising up leaders and releasing them to greater responsibility. *The Leadership Runway* is a map to a better future. I highly recommend it.

FRANK DAMAZIO, D.Min.
Chairman, Ministers Fellowship International (MFI)
Author, Mentor, Coach and Leadership Consultant.
Portland, Oregon, USA

Steve Murrell has always led, intending to leave someone else in charge. I have seen that first-hand in more than twenty-five years of working with him. This book contains not just an easy-to-read version of his dissertation but actual lessons from living what he is writing about. He shares both his failures and successes. Every ministry and every leader needs to have a clear transition and succession plan, and this book is your guide to preparing one.

PINKY C. KATIPUNAN
Lead Pastor, Victory Ortigas
Manila, Philippines

When Steve and I first met to explore his doctoral study, he was wrestling with one urgent fact: one day, a new chapter would unfold in the multinational organization he co-founded. If you take missional legacy seriously, if you are more concerned about the long-term success of those served through your mission than your own reputation, then you have been looking for Dr. Murrell's text.

RUSSELL W. WEST, Ph.D.
C-Suite Coach
Non-Profit Effectiveness Strategist
Nashville, Tennessee, USA

Steve Murrell, an outstanding Christian leader, has significantly impacted my life, family, and ministry. By teaching on and writing about the principles he's practiced for decades, he exemplifies what it looks like to be a disciple of the Lord Jesus Christ. This book will empower success, stability, and perpetuity in the great task of leadership transition and succession.

SAM AIYEDOGBON
Senior Apostolic Leader, Realm of Glory
International Churches
President, Global Peace and Social Justice Initiative
Lagos, Nigeria

It was once said, "The younger generation needs our shoulders, the older generation needs their eyes." Our values, their vision. The next five to ten years could bring the largest ministry transition in history. Experienced leaders will always have ministry options, but upcoming leaders will only come into their own when brought on by their elders. Be sensitive to the lifting of grace for your current ministry. Be willing to identify your successor. Thank you, Steve, for a lifetime of multiplication and transfer.

LARRY STOCKSTILL
Pastor, missionary, author, global church planter
Bethany Church
Baton Rouge, Louisiana, USA

Nations that were once thriving Christian communities now have church buildings that are empty and forgotten, largely due to the failure of churches, denominations, and pastors to transfer leadership to the next generation. As a third-generation pastor of a local church founded by my grandfather, I understand the importance of passing the baton of leadership in the right way. In *The Leadership Runway,* readers will find a Godsend that provides practical guidance for those seeking to do this well.

JONATHAN STOCKSTILL
Lead Pastor, Bethany Church
Baton Rouge, Louisiana, USA

Steve Murrell has written an important book on an incredibly important subject: healthy transitions. *The Leadership Runway* provides a practical and thoughtful paradigm for thinking through all aspects of the inevitable baton pass that every leader and ministry faces. I encourage every leader and leadership team to read and apply the wisdom offered in these pages.

LARRY OSBORNE, Ph.D.
Pastor, author, mentor, leadership consultant
North Coast Church
Vista, California, USA

Steve Murrell is an apostle of discipleship, whose strategies for leaders to secure a legacy cannot be underestimated. Drawing from his copious personal experience, leaders will glean so much from not only his teaching in this book, but also his life. Steve gives us all a clear pathway into the future.

PHIL PRINGLE
Pastor, author, artist
Founder, C3 Church Global
Sydney, Australia

Strategic leaders seamlessly and masterfully transition their leadership to the next generation at an epic juncture of their profession and calling. Steve Murrell created a hallmark of how success in ministry ensues from a commitment to an effective succession plan. Steve's insights, wisdom, and experience blend remarkably to deliver a brilliant blueprint for sustaining and scaling highly effective teams, organizations, and movements.

FARES ABRAHAM, DSL
Founder & CEO of Levant Ministries, USA
NEXTGEN Global Leader, Middle East and North Africa
Lake Mary, Florida, USA

In *The Leadership Runway,* Dr. Murrell offers invaluable insights on preparing emerging leaders, organizations, and experienced leaders for a successful handoff. Having served as both a senior pastor and ministry founder, I wish I had this resource when I prepared to pass my leadership baton years ago. If you're a CEO, pastor, or community leader, this book is a must-read to ensure a smooth transition and lasting success for your organization.

WAYNE HILSDEN, D.Min.
Co-Founder King of Kings Community, Jerusalem
Co-Founder of FIRM: Fellowship of Israel Related Ministries
Jerusalem, Israel

All who build something of substance intend it to prosper and last, but last how long? If built well, the endurance of the architecture should last beyond the architect. Dr. Steve Murrell has penned a seminal work on succession planning and execution. His contribution to this library of thought brings inestimable value to the reader.

BRETT FULLER
Bishop, Grace Covenant Church
Chaplain, Washington Commanders NFL team
Chairman, 2230: A House for the Nations
Washington, DC, USA

The Leadership Runway

A STRATEGY FOR MINISTRY SUCCESSION, LEADERSHIP TRANSITION, AND POST-FOUNDER SUSTAINABILITY

Steve Murrell

The Leadership Runway
Copyright © 2023 by Steve Murrell

Published by Every Nation Resources,
P.O. Box 1787. Brentwood, TN 37024-1787, USA.

All rights reserved. No portion of this book may be reproduced, stored in a retrieval system, or transmitted in any form or by any means—electronic, mechanical, photocopy, recording, scanning, or other—except for a brief quotation or in critical reviews or articles, without the prior written permission of the publisher.

Unless otherwise indicated, all Scripture quotations are from The ESV® Bible (The Holy Bible, English Standard Version®), copyright © 2001 by Crossway, a publishing ministry of Good News Publishers. Used by permission. All rights reserved.

Any internet addresses (websites, blogs, etc.) in this book are offered as a resource. They are not intended in any way to be or imply an endorsement by Every Nation Resources, nor does Every Nation Resources vouch for the content of these sites for the life of this book.

Library of Congress Cataloging-in-Publication Data:
Names: Murrell, Steve
Title: The Leadership Runway: A Strategy for Ministry Succession, Leadership Transition, and Post-Founder Sustainability
Subject: Leadership. | Christianity. | Ministry Succession.| Leadership Transition.
Print ISBN: 978-0-9752848-7-2
Ebook ISBN: 978-0-9752848-8-9

This book is dedicated to veteran pastors, missionaries, and ministry leaders who have served well and sacrificed much for the sake of the gospel and the success of the next generation.

"God is not unjust so as to overlook your work and the love that you have shown for his name in serving the saints, as you still do."

–Hebrews 6:10

Contents

Foreword

BY BISHOP EFRAIM TENDERO

A leader's legacy is measured by succession. Management guru Peter Drucker once said, "There is no success without a successor." In other words, lasting achievement is only fulfilled if it continues after we're gone. In order to secure a successful succession, we need a system that ensures continuous growth and sustainability by identifying and developing potential leaders to fill critical roles in the future. This is true both in secular business and in Christian ministry.

In the marketplace, a prime example is Steve Jobs, former CEO of Apple and founder of Apple University. At Apple, employees are taught "how to think like Steve Jobs and make decisions that he would make." This kind of training is key to the continuing growth and dominance of the Apple brand.

In the Bible, we have the successful examples of Moses preparing Joshua, Peter training John Mark, Paul equipping Timothy and others, and Jesus intentionally training his disciples. On the other hand, we also see an example of transition failure in the generation that followed Joshua. Judges 2:7 states, "And the people served the Lord all the days of Joshua, and all the days of the elders who outlived Joshua, who had seen all the great work that the Lord had done for Israel."

The next generation after Joshua's did not know the Lord or the work that he had done for Israel. It is appalling that they did what was evil in the sight of the Lord and served the Baals. They abandoned the Lord, the God of their fathers, who had brought them out of the land of Egypt.

Joshua and his colleagues did not employ a good succession plan. They failed to prepare the next generation, as reflected in Judges 2:12: "They went after other gods, from among the gods of the peoples who were around them and bowed down to them. And they provoked the Lord to anger."

Intentional succession planning is a must in Christian ministry. For this reason, Dr. Steve Murrell, the founder of Victory Church Manila and the cofounder of Every Nation Churches & Ministries, wrote *The Leadership Runway.*

What Dr. Murrell provides is an excellent combination of solid biblical principles, proven practices, clear strategies, and rich insights providing the reader with a helpful tool that not only will benefit one's ministry, but more importantly, will result in an empowered life. Rest assured, these principles and practices are not presented as dry, untested theory. No, Dr. Murrell illustrates these lessons through the lens of his own personal stories and experiences, detailing both successes and failures in his more than four decades of ministry.

As the National Director of the Philippine Council of Evangelical Churches, I was positioned to watch firsthand as Dr. Murrell and his team worked through the exemplary leadership transition processes outlined in *The Leadership Runway.* I can honestly say that they have demonstrated the principles and practices elucidated in this book.

Recently, Dr. Murrell invited me to address a cohort at Every Nation Seminary in Manila. In the open forum, a German pastor asked me, "What do you consider the big dangers and opportunities for the global church right now?" I explained that the challenges, particularly among evangelicals, are the megachurches. Too often, megachurches produce super-star pastors who become like messiahs, and their megachurch becomes like their own kingdoms. They end up expanding their own empires rather than the kingdom of God. This is a real problem.

By the grace of God, Victory and Every Nation have avoided this trap. Rather than building their own kingdom, Pastor Steve and the Victory Manila leaders modeled what it means to develop and empower emerging leaders. Pastor Steve shows throughout *The Leadership Runway* how he and his global Every Nation team have solidified these principles, sometimes by trial and error and sometimes through intentional development. As a result, they have experienced successful leadership transitions.

In the Philippines, Victory is an example of a thriving ministry that has successfully transitioned from a founder-leader church to a post-founder sustainable church. It is a megachurch of multiple congregations, yet they never lack emerging leaders who are highly qualified for biblical ministry. Why? They have consistently and intentionally invested in their upcoming, potential candidates.

Globally, Every Nation stands as an example of developing local-emerging leaders who are equipped to take on leadership roles as experienced leaders come in for their landing. It is also noteworthy that across generations, they have exhibited collegiality, camaraderie, and accountability with each other.

Fasten your seat belt, dear reader. Enjoy your journey in implementing the biblical principles and effective practices described and demonstrated in *The Leadership Runway.*

BISHOP EFRAIM TENDERO
Executive Director, Galilean Movement
Global Ambassador, World Evangelical Alliance

Preface

BY WILLIAM MURRELL

People often ask me what it was like to grow up in Victory Church Manila—one of the largest urban-megachurches in the world. I usually respond with a clarification and a question.

Clarification—it was not that big when I was there. I was born in 1986, two years into Victory's existence; and I moved away for university in 2005, just after the church's 20-year anniversary. It was Victory's exponential growth over the subsequent next two decades that would put Victory on the map of global evangelicalism as one of the most unique and rapidly growing churches in the world.

Question—"Which Victory?" I ask this question not only because Victory is a multi-site church (with congregations all over the densely populated metro area) but also because I was part of four different Victory congregations over my nineteen years in Manila—U-Belt (1986-1990), Makati (1990-1994), Ortigas (1994-2003), and Fort Bonifacio (2003-2005).

Growing up, I saw leadership transitions as normal (they occurred every 4-5 years in my childhood). It didn't occur to me as strange that the senior pastor of a growing church would leave the established one behind and start new congregations in new parts of the city—four times in twenty years. This often meant leaving some close friends behind, and twice it meant moving to a new house in a new part of the city.

It also meant new memories—the quirky kind often related to the meeting location of the new church.

For example, though I was only four when we left U-Belt, I vividly remember sneaking into my dad's office before church on Sunday mornings and grabbing a few donut holes ("munchkins") from the seemingly ever-present box from Dunkin' Donuts—yes, that Dunkin' Donuts.*

In Victory Makati, which met for many years in the ballroom of a sports club, I remember wandering over to the indoor tennis courts after service to watch people play tennis. This sport would later become my favorite and the inspiration for the Victory mantra: "same ole boring strokes."

At Victory Ortigas, which was Victory's first "mall church," I remember the Quickly cart where I had my first boba milk tea and would go on to get one every Friday before youth group—years before the Taiwanese delicacy became a fad in America.

And finally, at Victory BGC, I remember my quiet drives to church across an empty flat grassland called "Fort Bonifacio" that would be transformed in the next two decades from an old military base to a skyscraper-filled business district called Bonifacio Global City (or simply BGC). This is, fittingly, where Every Nation Seminary is currently headquartered.

For me, church transitions were normal and represented a new set of adventures and experiences. Whether I was 4 or 17, I looked forward to the change. I could not comprehend the risks and realities of church planting. New congregations simply meant new friends and new places to explore every Sunday.

---

* See Murrell, *100 Years from Now*, p. 23. "I vividly remember the day I sat down at my Dunkin' Donuts "office" in the heart of Manila's University Belt to write out the mission statement for this one-month-old Filipino church. On a Dunkin' Donuts napkin, I scribbled the first and most important words that came to mind: We exist to honor God..."

However, now that my wife and I are in the process of planting a church, I am beginning to remember my childhood differently. I'm beginning to reimagine what those years (1986-2005) must have been like for my parents. I'm trying to wrap my head around the level of risk and difficulty inherent in planting, establishing, growing, and then handing off, not one but four churches in 20 years.

For many pastors, it would be a lifetime accomplishment to successfully plant one church—to start from scratch and make disciples who make disciples over a sustained period of time. For others, the real accomplishment would be to plant a church that not only took root and thrived but succeeded and grew under subsequent leaders. These are worthy goals that many good leaders attempt and not all successfully accomplish.

Imagine doing it four times successfully before your 50th birthday.

For me, U-Belt is a reminder of my love for Dunkin' Donuts. For my parents, U-Belt is where the Miracle in Manila* began. It's the soul of Victory (and a model in Every Nation for church-based campus ministry). It was also my dad's first handoff in the Philippines—the first time he passed the baton to another senior leader. In this case, it was Luther Mancao. Under Luther's gifted leadership, Victory U-Belt doubled (from 600 to 1,200) in just three years. Today, CJ and Mye Nunag are serving as Victory U-Belt's sixth senior pastors. Under their leadership the church continues to grow in strength, depth, influence, and numbers. Thousands of Filipino students worship at one of seven weekly church services. Over 600 young disciple-makers lead small group discipleship on campuses and in dorms all over the U-Belt. And after nearly 40 years of existence, they recently purchased property a couple of blocks from our original U-Belt location. And yes, there is still a Dunkin' Donuts nearby.

It is a similar story for Makati, Ortigas, and the Fort.

---

* See Murrell, *100 Years from Now*, Chapter 2 on how Every Nation was founded.

Each transition was filled with risk, difficulty, and uncertainty, and they only look simple (even easy) in hindsight. In every case, the church thrived under the leadership of the succeeding pastor. And in every case, the church is still thriving under the leadership of the third, fourth, and in the case of U-Belt the sixth lead pastor.

In some sense, the Victory story is irreplicable.

In modern church history, one can find pastors leading churches growing exponentially, and one can find missionaries who are skilled at equipping and empowering local leaders. But it is exceedingly rare to find someone who successfully did both—especially at this scale and over a sustained period of time. Usually pastors of large megachurches struggle to find a successor. And usually missionaries who equip and empower locals do it on a relatively small scale—usually only once or twice in a lifetime. I do not know of any other church with so many successful leadership transitions over a sustained period of time. This success is ultimately a gift from God—a work of His Spirit in and through a local expression of His body. However, as was said of David in Psalm 78, for over 40 years my dad has led Victory (and later Every Nation) "with integrity of heart [and] with skillful hands."

This book represents not only four years of academic research on leadership transitions, but more importantly, four decades of loving and leading God's people well.

While the Victory story is irreplicable (and I'm convinced will be written about in church history books for many years to come), it is worthy of reflection and emulation. Wherever you are leading and whatever the scale, your leadership is temporary. All leaders leave. Every plane lands. So it's time we all begin thinking about leadership runways.

WILLIAM MURRELL, PH.D.
Academic Dean and Professor of Church History,
Every Nation Seminary

Introduction

The news media called it the "Miracle on the Hudson." A National Transportation Safety Board official called it "the most successful ditching in aviation history." Warner Bros. called it *Sully*—a movie directed by Clint Eastwood featuring Tom Hanks as Chesley "Sully" Sullenberger, the celebrated pilot.

On January 15, 2009, US Airways Flight 1549 departed New York City's LaGuardia Airport, bound for Charlotte, North Carolina. Almost immediately the Airbus A320 hit a flock of birds, causing the engine to lose power. Unable to get to an airport and with no other landing options, pilot Sully Sullenberger skillfully* landed on the frigid Hudson River. All 155 passengers and crew survived with few serious injuries. The pilots and crew deserved and received many honors for their heroism in this near-death situation.

Key lessons of this story are easily applied to ministry succession and sustainability. Pilots never want to crash a plane. Similarly, pastors never want to crash a church. But many in ministry do just that when they retire (or die) without a succession plan or a successor. In the context of ministry succession, leadership transition, and post-founder sustainability, two lessons from the "Miracle on the Hudson" must not be overlooked.

First, while a highly skilled pilot can sometimes land a plane with no runway and without killing passengers, most people

---

* "Miraculously" according to many.

cannot. The surprising fact that no one died in the Hudson River landing is why Sully has been called a hero and the river landing has been called a "miracle." Sully's "miraculous" water landing did not prompt the airline industry to conclude that runways are no longer necessary. Applied to ministry, this means that while some highly gifted leaders can instinctively (or luckily) land a ministry plane without a runway (or do leadership transition without a succession plan), most cannot. Runways are still necessary for safe landings, and succession plans are still necessary for healthy ministry transitions. Unfortunately, many ministers attempt to land their ministry with no leadership runway in sight, and they seem to expect their successors to gain altitude without a runway. When we take the time to build a leadership runway (succession plan and leadership transition strategy), most emerging leaders will gain altitude faster and most experienced leaders will land safer.

Second, while the famous Hudson River landing was successful in terms of saving lives, the US Airways plane was destroyed in the crash and never flew again. In a ministry context, that would be like a leadership transition where individual leaders survived, but the church or ministry didn't.

This book aims to provide experienced and emerging ministry leaders with the tools to develop a strategic succession plan and, more importantly, the wisdom to turn that plan into a smooth leadership transition—one that results in a ministry that not only survives but thrives with next-generation leadership.

Back to School

In 2016, after 35 years of vocational ministry and knowing that I couldn't lead forever, I went back to school specifically to study post-founder sustainability in the context of a global ministry. I was 57 years old when my first class started and 60 when I graduated. I went back to school, not to get another degree, but to actually learn something. I knew generally what I needed to learn, and Asbury Theological Seminary's Doctor of Ministry program seemed perfect for my quest.

During my three years as an Asbury student, I read, studied, researched, and wrote about post-founder ministry sustainability every day. For those three years, I woke up thinking about post-founder sustainability and went to bed thinking about post-founder sustainability. My research quickly led me to succession planning, leadership transition, and a myriad of other related topics. To no one's surprise, my dissertation was titled: "Post-Founder Sustainability: Building Ministries that Outlive Their Founders."

Dissertations (aka "theses" in the UK and South Africa) are an odd genre of literature—academic writing designed to be read by the small committee of scholars who decide if the writer has used enough big words and impressive endnotes to earn another degree. No one reads a dissertation unless they are a professor assigned to the committee or a doctoral student needing one more reference for their own dissertation documentation.

This book is an attempt to transform three years of dissertation research and writing into something that will be useful and readable for leaders who do not live in an academic ivory tower. Specifically, I hope this book helps pastors and ministry leaders understand the process and urgency of succession planning and leadership transition.

The purpose of my dissertation research was to discover why some denominations, mission organizations, and megachurches achieve post-founder sustainability and to determine next steps for succession planning and leadership transition in Every Nation Churches & Ministries.

As I write, I'm thinking about the 66-year-old founding pastor of a 35-year-old church who feels it is time to "pass the leadership baton" but is not sure if the designated successor is ready. I am thinking about his successor who is unsure what parts of church structure can be changed and what parts cannot once he becomes the senior leader. I'm thinking about the faithful cross-cultural missionary couple who spent a lifetime learning a new language, engaging an unfamiliar culture, and developing indigenous leaders. The locals are ready to lead, and it is time for the missionaries to transition to the next phase of ministry. But what does the next step look like for that veteran missionary couple? I am thinking about the campus ministry regional director who has been successful at every level of campus ministry, but now feels called to plant a new church. How will she identify and develop her replacement? How will she prepare for a pastoral ministry role?

Why This Book?

The goal of this book is more than a well-written succession plan. Succession planning is important, and will be addressed, but a well-written succession plan does not guarantee a smooth leadership transition. My prayer is that this book will equip leadership teams to formulate useful succession plans *and* facilitate successful leadership transitions. The ultimate goal is for leadership transition to be done in a way that will not only enable ministry survival, but also empower ministry multiplication.

Three years of dissertation research unearthed a three-part pattern in successful leadership transitions that was confirmed by multiple sources, both in ministry and business literature. Here are the non-negotiable big three requirements for successful succession:

1. Prepare emerging leaders to lead the organization.

2. Prepare the organization to be led by emerging leaders.

3. Prepare experienced leaders to finish well.

The Leadership Runway is organized around these three principles. When all three are understood and applied, the possibility of a successful leadership transition increases. When one or more is neglected, the possibility of a runway crash increases.

About the Title

As I was preparing to write this book, I discovered many airline stories, similar to the "Miracle on the Hudson," that provide applicable illustrations for leadership transition—both good and bad. I am thankful for the staff in Every Nation's Nashville office who helped me connect the dots between these two topics, resulting in *The Leadership Runway* as the title. The book's subtitle, *A Strategy for Ministry Succession, Leadership Transition, and Post-Founder Sustainability* simply describes what this book offers.

Since most chapters reference my runway metaphor, perhaps the following examples will help explain why aviators (and spiritual leaders) need runways.

Refuel. This is the most common reason that aircraft land. Every plane needs to refuel. While it is possible to refuel in the air, most refueling is done on the ground. There is danger in ignoring the refuel signs. Likewise, while it is possible for ministers to refuel on the job, it is usually necessary to land in order to refuel. There is grave danger when a minister leads on empty. The leadership runway is a place where pastors and spiritual leaders can land to refuel. There is nothing wrong with a plane landing to refuel, and there is nothing wrong with a spiritual leader taking time out to refuel.

Redirect. Every day, planes land, take new passengers, and redirect to a new destination. Sometimes, dangerous weather patterns necessitate the redirect. In ministry, landing to redirect is common. Sometimes the redirect is due to dangers ahead. In other cases, it is simply time to pass the leadership baton to someone else and move on to another place of ministry. The leadership runway is designed for experienced and emerging leaders to get new direction and new marching orders.

Retool. Periodically, jet planes land in order to upgrade and retool. Experienced ministers also need to land in order to upgrade and retool for the next season of leadership. Because this one feels the least urgent, it tends to get neglected by ministry leaders.

Repair. When something is broken and needs to be fixed, the pilot must land. If a pilot ignores the need for repair, many people are put in danger. Applied to ministry, there are times spiritual leaders need repair, restoration, refreshing, and revival. Spiritual leaders who refuse to land for soul repair and restoration put themselves and others in danger.

Retire. In all of the above situations, the pilot lands the plane in order to take off again, but in a better, stronger condition. Retirement is different. The retired aircraft is still valuable, but it will never fly again. Sometimes this is the case with ministry retirement, especially when a leader retires because of health reasons. They will often never fly again because they are physically or mentally unable. But in most ministry situations retirement is not the end of ministry. It is not uncommon for an experienced ministry leader to retire from one position or organization, only to take off on the leadership runway in a different role or location.

If a pilot ignores the need to refuel, redirect, retool, or repair and refuses to land, disaster is inevitable. Likewise, for the minister who ignores the need to refuel, redirect, retool, or repair and refuses to land, disaster is inevitable.

After this explanation, some of you may be wondering what ministry retirement means. What does it look like for a man or woman who still feels the call to ministry, but not to their current position? Three aspects of ministry retirement will be addressed in chapters 11, 12, and 13.

Because No One Leads Forever

I am often asked why I talk, preach, and write about ministry succession planning and leadership transition so much. In *NEXT: Pastoral Succession that Works,* ministry consultants William Vanderbloemen and Warren Bird answer that question succinctly:

> Every pastor is an interim pastor. Few ministers consider that truth. Few are eager to admit that their time with their present church will one day end. But ultimately, all pastors are "interim" because the day when a successor takes over will come for everyone in ministry. Planning for that day of succession may be the biggest leadership task a leader and church will ever face. It may also be the most important.[1]

In other words, understanding succession planning and leadership transition is important because no one leads forever.

May this book help you do succession planning wisely and leadership transition humbly, so that your ministry will not crash-land but will multiply and thrive 100 years from now.

As we prepare to take off, it is time to fasten your seatbelts, fold up your tray tables, put your seats in the upright position, turn off all electronic devices, throw your carry-on junk under the seat, and get ready to soar!

The Leadership Runway

In the early years of creating their flying machine, Orville and Wilbur Wright regularly traveled from Dayton, Ohio, to the beaches of Kitty Hawk, North Carolina, because wind from the Atlantic Ocean powered the takeoff and the sand dunes softened the crash landing. In those days runways did not exist. Pioneers like the Wright brothers were too focused on flying to worry about landing. Their wind-powered gliders simply crash-landed wherever they happened to be when the wind stopped.

Aviators eventually recognized the need for runways—spaces specifically designed for successful takeoff and safe landing. From sand, to dirt and then to pavement, each runway iteration was an upgrade. Just as well-designed runways were an afterthought in the development of aviation, succession plans are too often afterthoughts in the ministry world.

Part I of *The Leadership Runway* is designed to introduce, explain, and apply the runway metaphor to ministry succession so that it will no longer be an afterthought, but an urgent task. The first three chapters address the necessity of succession planning, the danger of haphazard leadership transition, and the power of Christian institutions.

CHAPTER 1

Avoiding Runway Disasters

Runway: a defined rectangular area on a land aerodrome prepared for the landing and takeoff of aircraft.

–International Civil Aviation Organization

After my departure, fierce wolves will come in among you, not sparing the flock.

–Apostle Paul, Acts 20:29

The deadliest accident in aviation history happened on a runway, not in the air.

In the late 1970s, Jacob Veldhuyzen van Zanten was a celebrity pilot, the face of KLM Royal Dutch Airlines. Photos of Captain Veldhuyzen van Zanten in full uniform appeared in magazine travel ads. Along with being a KLM pilot and pitchman, he also served as the head of KLM's flight training department and chief flight instructor for their 747 pilots.

He was an experienced professional at the top of his game, yet his pilot error caused the worst airline accident in history.

The captain's last words, "We gaan" (Let's go), were captured on the cockpit recorder on March 27, 1977, a few seconds before his KLM 747 crashed into a Pan Am 747 at Los Rodeos Airport on Tenerife Island. Neither plane was supposed to be on that runway or on that island. But because of a terrorist bomb explosion at Gran Canaria Airport, both planes and their 644 passengers and crew were diverted to this small airport off the coast of West Africa.

All 248 passengers and crew aboard KLM's 747 died instantly, incinerated in the fiery explosion. The Pan Am 747 lost 335 passengers with 61 survivors. The final death toll was 583.

Multiple factors contributed to the Tenerife Island disaster.

- Diverted flights caused *over-crowded runways*.
- Unexpected weather patterns forced *last-minute decisions*.
- Heavy fog produced *impaired vision*.
- The lack of standardized language created *confused communication*.

Taking all of that and more into account, the 70-member team of Spanish, Dutch, and American aviation investigators concluded that the main culprit was pilot error. The investigators laid the blame at the feet of KLM's most celebrated senior pilot, Captain Jacob Veldhuyzen van Zanten.

In a church and ministry context, over-crowded runways, last-minute decisions, impaired vision, and confused communication often lead to "pastor error" and ministry transition disasters. Most ministry runway disasters can be avoided if we build better succession runways, eliminate last-minute transition decisions, clarify vision, and overcommunicate.

PILOT ERROR AND RUNWAY DISASTERS

Because we tend to think that speed and height are dangerous, it might surprise you that the low and slow part of a flight is actually more dangerous and deadly than the high and fast part. Low and slow refers to the takeoff and landing phase and represents only a small portion of the actual flight time. Even on short flights, much more time is spent high and fast than low and slow. In terms of accidental aviation fatalities, 49% happen during landing and 14% during takeoff. That means 63% of fatalities happen during the low and slow phase—on or near the runway—and only 37% occur while the plane is high and fast.

I can't prove it with data, but my experience tells me similar percentages might also apply to leadership transition crashes in churches and ministries. If we can get the plane off the runway and high in the air, there is less chance of a fatal crash. Likewise, if we can get the leader firmly in the pilot seat with hands on the controls, there is a better chance of a successful ministry. Whether we are taking off or landing, the runway (succession and transition) is the danger zone.

Before we start building our leadership runway, let's take a moment to consider the most common causes of runway disasters. When the Tenerife Island runway disaster was analyzed, the challenging circumstances were obvious—over-crowded runways, last-minute decisions, impaired vision, and confused communication—but the real problem was pilot error. Every runway disaster is unique, but like Tenerife Island, most are ultimately caused by pilot error. Likewise, in the church world, every leadership transition is unique and challenging, but the most common fatal flaw is "pastor error."

The aviation industry has identified three common pilot errors that lead to runway disasters: incursion, excursion, and confusion.

Runway Incursion

According to the International Civil Aviation Organization, a runway incursion happens when an unauthorized aircraft, vehicle, or person is on the runway that an authorized aircraft is attempting to use for its takeoff or landing. The danger this creates is obvious.

Though I had never heard the phrase "runway incursion," I almost experienced one on my first flight from Manila's massive international airport to Baguio City's small provincial airport. After the short 114 nautical mile flight (211 km), as our pilot was landing the 16-seat prop plane on the mountain runway, I looked out of my window and thought I saw cattle being herded across the runway. I was informed later by a friend who lived about 100 meters from the runway that there is a designated person whose main job is to herd all cows, goats, pigs, and other animals (both wild and domestic) from the runway before takeoff and landing. If that Baguio cowboy had failed to do his job, I might have experienced my own bovine runway incursion.

In a ministry context, someone must make sure the runway is clear as experienced leaders are landing and emerging leaders are taking off. On more than one occasion, I have been the leader who is landing and getting out of the way so a new leader could take off. In my experience as the outgoing leader, I was usually the one with the unwritten responsibility to clear the runway of myself, my peers, and my traditions so the new leaders could take off incursion free. There have also been numerous times when I had to clear the runway so older leaders could land safely—sometimes to redirect, refuel, retool, or refresh, and other times to retire to the control tower in a coaching role. Either way, the runway must be cleared of aircraft, vehicles, people, goats, pigs, and sacred cows that might get in the way of a safe landing or takeoff. If the runway is not cleared, a fatal ministry crash is a real possibility.

Runway Excursion

The Federal Aviation Administration describes a runway excursion as "a veer off or overrun from the runway surface." Unlike an incursion, which involves other aircraft or vehicles, an excursion is a single aircraft accident. The most common excursion is an "overrun," which happens when the runway ends before the plane stops.

Overrun is unfortunately common in ministry leadership transitions. The emerging leader is ready to take off. But the experienced leader, who is supposed to go low and slow in order to land, decides to hit the accelerator rather than the brakes. You can imagine the tragic results when a leader runs out of runway before he has fully stopped. To fully stop does not necessarily mean full and immediate retirement, but it does mean to fully stop doing the job that the new leader has been tasked to do. Two leaders in the driver's seat at the same time does not work. If you are an experienced leader who is considering landing, remember: the goal is to come to a full stop before the runway ends.

Runway "undershoot" is a less common type of excursion. This is the opposite of the overrun. Undershoot means the pilot attempts to land the plane before the runway starts. In a ministry context, this happens when an experienced leader quits, retires, or moves on to another ministry role before the emerging leader is ready to lead the organization or before the organization is ready to be led by the new leader. A healthy leadership transition requires strategic teamwork. Unfortunately, some leaders move on without doing the hard work to ensure a good transition.

Runway Confusion

Whether during takeoff, landing, or taxiing, the problem of runway confusion happens when an aircraft uses the wrong runway. This confusion can cause disastrous contact with another aircraft, an airport vehicle, or humans.

In the ministry world, runway confusion is often the result of not having a written succession plan, or not clearly communicating the written plan to all who are involved. When the experienced leader is on the same runway at the same time as the emerging leader, we have runway confusion. A well-written succession plan will clarify which runway each leader should be on. The best solution to ministry runway confusion is clear writing and constant communication. *

SPIRITUAL WARFARE AND SUCCESSION PLANNING**

As important as written strategic clarity is, it would be naive to ignore the spiritual warfare aspect of leadership transition, especially in a church or ministry context. Scripture is filled with stories of disruptive human and demonic activity during times of leadership transition. Similarly, we also see examples of human encouragement and angelic visitations in those same transition narratives. As we look briefly at three familiar leadership transitions in the New Testament—John the Baptist to Jesus, Jesus to the Twelve, and Paul to the Ephesus Elders—notice the presence and activity of devils, angels, and the Holy Spirit. No matter our opinions on spiritual warfare or demonology, we would be wise to accept the fact that leadership transition in ministry will always be

---

* Unfortunately, sometimes the problem is not confusion, but a refusal to abide by the succession plan.

** For further discussion and biblical examples of demonic spiritual warfare and angelic help during leadership transitions, see Appendix C: "Leadership Transitions and Spiritual Warfare."

accompanied by a new level of human and spiritual opposition, as well as a fresh presence and power of the Holy Spirit.*

Along with the spiritual warfare aspect of transition, four biblical principles are foundational to healthy ministry leadership transitions.

1. The Decrease Principle

As John the Baptist's leadership transition approached, he confessed, "I must decrease" (John 3:30). These three powerful words describe the ideal attitude of a leader who is transitioning out of a leadership position and clearing the runway for the next leader. The context of this text is important. The disciples of John were complaining that many of their disciples were starting to follow Jesus. Their crowds were steadily shrinking, while Jesus' crowds were rapidly growing. Their beloved leader's influence seemed to be decreasing, and they were not happy about that at all.

The John-to-Jesus leadership transition exposed insecurities in the hearts and attitudes of John's inner circle. John's reply to them was the polar opposite of insecurity:

"I am not the Christ."

"He must increase."

"I must decrease."

I often advise experienced spiritual leaders, especially those who are leading growing ministries, to look in the mirror and speak the words of John: "I am not the Christ. He must increase. I must decrease."

"I am not the Christ" is a reminder that I am not the ultimate leader of whatever I am responsible to lead. "He must increase" has a dual meaning—that Christ must increase in my life and that emerging leaders must increase in my ministry. "I must decrease" is a reminder that no leader leads forever, and if we want to avoid a

---

* Or as my prophetic friends like to say, "New levels, new devils."

runway crash, we must intentionally decrease. Decrease does not mean disappear. In most leadership transition situations, a gradual decrease is much better than a sudden disappearance.

I have talked to many leaders who struggle with the concept of decreasing because they assume that "decrease" means retirement. Visionary leaders are not the type of people who dream of retiring to the golf course. On the contrary, high-octane leaders dream of pioneering and producing until their funeral, and maybe beyond. The problem occurs when established leaders refuse to embrace the decrease principle. Thinking that they can lead forever, they inadvertently block the "increase" in the lives of the next generation.

(The Decrease Principle is so important in ministry succession that I have written a whole chapter on the principle. See Chapter 12: "I Must Decrease").

2. The Temptation Principle

The second principle of healthy leadership transition tells us that we should expect temptation from invisible non-human beings. We should also expect the help of the Holy Spirit and angles.

The Decrease Principle describes what is required of an *experienced* leader who is in the process of landing on the runway. The Temptation Principle describes the same runway, but from the perspective of the *emerging* leader who is speeding down the runway, attempting to take off.

As Jesus was about to start his public ministry, the Apostle John wrote, "Jesus was led up by the Spirit into the wilderness to be tempted by the devil" (Matthew 4:1). In other words, major leadership transitions means major temptations, new authority means new temptations, greater responsibilities means greater temptations, and increased visibility means increased temptations. Pilots know that most airline disasters happen on or just above the runway, not at 30,000 feet in the air. Likewise, the devil knows that the leadership transition period is the most precarious and dangerous, so he consistently shows up when established leaders are attempting to land and emerging leaders are attempting to take off. His goal is a runway disaster.

Matthew continues his narrative, "Then the devil left him, and behold, angels came and were ministering to him" (Matthew 4:11). Maybe this also happens in corporate leadership transitions, but devils and angels both tend to get involved in church and ministry leadership transitions. Ministry leaders would be wise to acknowledge the spiritual warfare aspect of succession planning and leadership transition, and foolish to ignore it.

Notice in Luke's parallel account that along with devils and angels, we find the Holy Spirit right in the center of this spiritual conflict. According to Luke, Jesus was "full of the Spirit" and "led by the Spirit" before the epic battle with Satan. After the spiritual battle was won and the leadership transition complete, "Jesus returned in the power of the Spirit" (Luke 4:1-14). No matter how wise our succession plan, being Spirit-filled, Spirit-led, and Spirit-empowered is essential for successful ministry succession.

3. The Savage Wolf Principle

While the previous point dealt with the devil bringing temptation, the Savage Wolf Principle has to do with relational conflict and theological confusion caused by people. In Acts 20, as Paul communicated to the Ephesian elders that he was departing and would never see them again, he warned that "fierce wolves" from the outside and "twisted" teachings from the inside would seek to harm the flock. Paul warned the elders, "I know that after my departure, fierce wolves will come in among you, not sparing the flock" (Acts 20:29). From Paul's epistles written in the following years, we know that his concerns were valid. Fierce wolves did come in from the outside bringing theological controversy and false teachers did emerge on the inside bringing relational conflict.*

These metaphorical wolves were evil, but not stupid. They were smart enough to delay their attack until after the experienced leader's departure. That's still their strategy today. As soon as the experienced leader transitions out, the fierce wolves creep in. They know that they will be more successful when they attack younger less-experienced leaders.

Along with fierce wolves attacking from the outside, Paul also warned about internal attacks: "**From among your own selves** will arise men speaking twisted things, to draw away the disciples after them" (Acts 20:30). Twisted teachings are especially insidious because they are an attack from insiders. Teachers who twist Scripture are easily identified by their narcissistic tendency to "draw away disciples after them" rather than leading disciples to Jesus and the church community.

Because twisted teachers are insiders, their opposition feels like a personal attack, and thus are more painful than attacks from fierce wolves who are usually anonymous outsiders. To put it in a modern context, I care what my friends and colleagues say about me, but I care very little what online influencers say about me. Part of succession preparation is preparing the heart for the pain of unexpected insider betrayal.

When human dysfunction or demonic conflict happens during a leadership transition, the tendency is to focus on the people who are behaving like fierce wolves and twisted teachers. However, in the midst of transition conflict, Paul reminded the elders that "the Holy Spirit has made you overseers, to care for the church of God." The job of the emerging spiritual leaders during transition is "to care for" God's church, not to focus on fierce wolves and obsess over twisted teaching. The foundational starting point to effective spiritual leadership during transition is to know that "the Holy

---

* For example, see 1 Timothy 6.

Spirit has made you overseers." This goes straight to the idea of vocational ministry calling.* If we know God has called us to lead this flock at this time, then we also know that God has graced and gifted us to lead this flock at this time.

As we've seen, Acts 20 contains Paul's apostolic warning along with wise instruction to emerging leaders during the Ephesus leadership transition. Verse 30 warns of internal divisions through twisted teachings. Verse 29 warns of external attacks from fierce wolves. Verse 28 is the four-fold wisdom emerging leaders need to act on: "Pay careful attention to yourselves and to all the flock, in which the Holy Spirit has made you overseers, to care for the church of God."

If you are an emerging leader, here's my summary of Paul's warning and wisdom when transition conflict happens:

Guard your heart. On every flight, passengers are instructed, in the case of change in cabin pressure, to secure their own oxygen masks before assisting others. Similarly, Paul instructed emerging leaders, in the case of wolves and twisters, to "Pay careful attention to yourselves." This is not a self-absorbed narcissism, but a serious guarding of the heart.

Focus on your flock. In every transition, the first leadership move is to guard your own heart, the second is not to obsess over the wolf, but to focus on the flock. "Pay careful attention... to all the flock."

Remember your calling. Paul reminded the Ephesian elders that "the Holy Spirit has made you overseers." In times of transition and crisis, it always helps me to remind myself that my oversight position was the Holy Spirit's idea, not mine.

Do your job. Your primary job is not to wrestle wolves or untwist the twisted, but to "Care for the church of God."

---

* See Chapter 7: "Perceiving Sacred Calling."

Both external and internal spiritual attacks increase during leadership transition for churches and missions organizations. The devil will do everything he can to disrupt safe landings and successful takeoffs in the hope of causing fatal crashes on our leadership runways. The leadership runway succession strategy will not diminish or eliminate fierce wolves and twisted teachings; but hopefully, it will help experienced and emerging leaders prepare for the common relational conflicts and intense spiritual warfare that so often accompanies ministry succession.

Our fourth and final succession principle is a proven tool for defeating demonic powers every time.

4. The Sacrifice Principle

The fourth principle of healthy ministry leadership transition relies on experienced leaders sacrificing for the benefit of emerging leaders.

Just as Jesus experienced increased spiritual conflict during the leadership transition from John the Baptist to him, he also experienced intense spiritual warfare as he began to transition leadership to his disciples. As Jesus decreased so the twelve could increase, human and demonic attacks intensified. The once-in-history leadership transition from Jesus to his disciples included the agony of Gethsemane, the betrayal of Judas, the denial of Peter, and the injustice of the cross.*

Emotional agony, relational conflict, and unexpected suffering are not uncommon experiences during ministry transitions. Therefore, it is wise to plan for the worst and hope for the best during high-level leadership transitions. To put it simply: don't be surprised; be ready.

---

* Obviously, Gethsemane and Golgotha represent much more to the Christian faith than leadership transition principles. Nevertheless, on a secondary level, a leadership transition from Jesus to his original apostles was happening while Jesus was making the ultimate sacrifice for the sins of humanity.

THE LEADERSHIP RUNWAY

The purpose of *The Leadership Runway* is to help emerging leaders and experienced leaders understand the importance of ministry succession planning and to help experienced leaders build a contextualized succession plan. Our two-fold outcome objective is to build a leadership runway that will empower new leaders to take off safely, then soar high and fly fast, and to provide a safe low and slow landing place for leaders who need to refuel, retool, repair, redirect, or retire.*

This chapter started with the tragic story of the deadliest accident in aviation history. The ensuing investigation discovered that, despite the extenuating circumstances, the runway disaster was due to pilot error. Surprisingly, the pilot charged with the fatal error was not a rookie, but an extremely experienced pilot. Since ministry leadership transition is usually primarily in the hands of experienced leaders, not novices, most ministry transition crash landings are caused by senior pastor error.

As we examined New Testament leadership transitions, multiple biblical principles emerged that, when incorporated into succession plans, will help us avoid pilot error and runway crashes.

While we accept that ministry succession always involves misguided humans, demonic opposition, along with supernatural help, our confidence should not rest in a succession plan, but in being filled with, led by, and empowered by the Holy Spirit.

---

* See Chapter 11: "Is My Ministry Still Needed?"

Admitting My Greatest Leadership Failure

*I had to take complete ownership of what went wrong.
That is what a leader does—even if it means getting fired.
If anyone was to be blamed and fired for what happened,
let it be me. Leaders must own everything in their world.
There is no one else to blame.*

—Jocko Willink, Extreme Ownership

*The fire will test what sort of work each one has done. If
the work that anyone has built on the foundation survives,
he will receive a reward. If anyone's work is burned up, he
will suffer loss, though he himself will be saved, but only
as through fire.*

—Apostle Paul, 1 Corinthians 3:13-15

Tiny regional airports near sleepy college towns are rarely mentioned in the national news. But on August 8, 2015, when Moe and his fiancé, Jaelyn, were arrested by the FBI at the Golden Triangle Regional Airport 26 miles north of Mississippi State University (MSU), the national media took note. This was a big story, not only for a tiny town in northeast Mississippi, but for the USA.

When Moe and Jaelyn met 10 months before that life-changing and life-saving day, they were MSU students studying psychology (Moe) and chemistry (Jaelyn).

During her trial, it was revealed in a letter to her family that Jaelyn took full responsibility. "It was all my planning—I found the contacts, made arrangements, planned the departure, I am guilty of what you soon will find out." In another letter, she confessed to being "fully aware of the consequences of my actions, should I be caught."

Their plan was to take the Delta flight from Columbus, Mississippi, to Istanbul, Turkey, via Atlanta and Amsterdam. In Istanbul, they would meet their recruiter, at the Sultan Ahmed Mosque,* in order to receive final instructions before departing for Syria.

Their mission in Syria was jihad.

On March 13, 2016, Moe pleaded guilty to "conspiring to provide material support" to ISIS, a terrorist organization. His sentence included 8 years in a federal prison, followed by 15 years of supervised release. Two weeks later, Jaelyn pleaded guilty and was sentenced to 12 years in federal prison followed by 15 years of probation. Moe received leniency because he cooperated with the FBI. Jaelyn did not.

Upon receiving his sentence, Moe reportedly thanked the FBI agents for saving his life. Years later, during an interview in prison, Moe said he was relieved to get caught before boarding that

---

*The Blue Mosque

plane in Columbus, acknowledging that he probably would have died in Syria.

Jaelyn expressed no such sentiment, at least not on the record.

An unlikely jihadist, Jaelyn Young grew up in a Christian home in Vicksburg, Mississippi, the daughter of a US Navy veteran turned police officer. While in the navy, her father served multiple tours of duty in Iraq and Afghanistan. He stated that his daughter often begged him not to go away. He explained to the judge, "I had a moral obligation to my country." Jaelyn's mother was a school superintendent. Jaelyn was a scholar and a cheerleader. An article in *The Atlantic* described her as "nerdy enough to join the National Honor Society and Mu Alpha Theta math club, but cool enough to be on the homecoming court twice."

The Young family attended Triumph Church, a multicultural church in Vicksburg, Mississippi, connected with ARC (Association of Related Churches). To the shock of her family and friends, Jaelyn converted to Islam in her second year at Mississippi State University and started attending the Islamic Center on 204 Herbert Street, near the MSU campus.

Remember that address: 204 Herbert Street. As the painful story of my greatest leadership failure unfolds, Herbert Street will become a silent witness to that failure.

In the fall of 2014, Jaelyn and Moe had become friends and were spending more and more time together. By March 2015, Jaelyn confessed the *shahada*—the Muslim profession of faith: "There is no god but Allah, and Muhammad is his messenger." From that day forward, it was obvious that Jaelyn was all in. Her hunger to learn and live the Quran provoked Moe to go beyond his surface-level religious commitment and lead her to the radical edge of her new faith. Just five months later, they were willing to sacrifice everything—including their lives—to support the Caliphate and join the jihad.

Muhammed Dakhlalla (Moe) was born and raised in Starkville, Mississippi, the son of a Palestinian immigrant who was originally from Bethlehem in the West Bank. Moe's mother was an American convert to Islam from New Jersey who was known in the city and on the MSU campus for her baking skills, especially her bread. Moe did not grow up in a radicalized Muslim family. He was just as unlikely a jihadist as Jaelyn.[1]

A MIRACLE ON HERBERT STREET

In four decades of ministry, I have been on both ends of leadership transitions—appointing a successor and being appointed as a successor. Most of my succession experiences ended well. Some did not. To use the overarching metaphor of this book, never was a leadership transition such a disastrous runway crash-landing as when I left Starkville, Mississippi, to follow God's call to Manila, Philippines. It was not an immediate crash. It was a slow-motion crash, but nonetheless, a total runway disaster.

The sad story of Moe and Jaelyn is directly connected to my leadership transition failure and to a building on 206 Herbert Street, next door to the Islamic Center—the Dakhlalla home—on 204 Herbert Street.

It was the fall of 1977, and I was a freshman business major at Mississippi State University. My main goal and prayer the first week had nothing to do with classes, professors, or grades. I needed to find Christian fellowship. I was a relatively new believer, and I didn't know much, but I did know that my fledgling faith would not survive one semester if I didn't find a faith community. God answered my prayers, and in my first week on the MSU campus, I met a campus missionary named Walter Walker who invited me to a Bible study for students. I was one of eight people at that first meeting near campus. The next week, I invited my roommates.

A year later, an accounting student named Rice Broocks wandered into one of Walter's Bible studies. That night, Rice had a life-changing encounter with God, and instantly, our little student ministry started to grow. Students were getting saved almost every week—athletes, international students, grad students. What had been a small group of middle-class white students before Rice arrived quickly became a multiethnic ministry including Latinos, Asians, African Americans, and West Africans. We were probably the most diverse student group on the MSU campus. That's what happens when a young evangelist gets right with God, understands the gospel, and boldly shares his faith with everyone he meets!

Because of this growth, we needed a larger facility. As soon as we started praying and searching, Walter discovered that the ATO fraternity house located on 206 Herbert Street was up for sale. The ATO frat house was next door to the Dakhlalla home, which doubled as the Islamic Center on 204 Herbert Street.

This frat house was exactly what we needed. It was the perfect location to reach Mississippi State University students and had plenty of room for Bible studies, worship services, and a dorm-like environment to house students who desired Christian community. But there was a problem, a huge problem. We had no money. We were a tiny student church with a big vision and a small budget. No banker with a functioning brain would ever consider giving us a loan, but that did not stop Walter from trying. Of course, every bank in Starkville said no.

We prayed and asked God to do a miracle. And he did. Thanks to generous help from Rice's parents, we were able to purchase that fraternity house and transform it into a student ministry center. The ground floor became a multi-function worship auditorium with an industrial kitchen attached. The basement and third floors became dormitories for MSU students who wanted Christian community.

I lived in that big ministry house, along with Rice and a dozen other young men, for a couple of years. We had weekly worship services, daily prayer meetings, constant discipleship groups, and countless baptisms. God was honored and lives were changed. For years, the fraternity house on 206 Herbert Street had been the address of alcohol-drenched college frat parties; it was now the address of an outpouring of the Holy Spirit.

As soon as Rice graduated, he hit the road as an itinerant campus evangelist, hopping from campus to campus, preaching the gospel, and planting churches. A year later, Walter and his family moved to Nebraska to start a new ministry at the University of Nebraska, and I was appointed the leader of the small campus church that was meeting on 206 Herbert Street.

After leading that campus ministry and student church for two years as a clueless single man, I got married and led for another two years along with my wife, Deborah. We were planning to spend the rest of our lives in Starkville reaching Mississippi State University students with the gospel. We were content and life was good.

In terms of the leadership runway succession strategy, Walter and Linda Walker had succeeded. The MSU student church they started was small, but healthy. They passed the leadership baton to me and moved to another state to pioneer a new campus church. The leadership transition had worked. Well done, Walter and Linda! For the next few years, our campus ministry and student church gradually grew stronger, more diverse, and a little larger under my leadership.

A MOSQUE ON HERBERT STREET

In 1984, after a one-month mission trip to Manila's University-Belt, Deborah and I felt called to the Philippines, which meant that we would be leaving the Starkville church behind. So we gathered our little student church in that former fraternity house on 206 Herbert

Street and promised they would soon meet their new pastor (who was sure to be as poorly equipped and unprepared as me). We emphasized that although we were going to Asia, the mission to the MSU campus would continue right here in this place—in this very building that God had miraculously given to us. In our view, 206 Herbert Street was holy ground, set aside for prayer, worship, and discipleship. Yes, the MSU mission would continue even though we were being called to the other side of the planet.

We sincerely believed that.

We were sincerely wrong.

After packing a couple of suitcases, putting everything else we owned in storage, and emptying our bank account to purchase plane tickets, we flew back to the Philippines. We landed in Manila on November 30, 1984, and immediately threw ourselves into student discipleship and leadership development.

During our first year in Manila, our church and campus ministry was gradually growing larger and stronger. Meanwhile back in Mississippi, the MSU ministry seemed to be doing okay.

Then it wasn't.

Within two years of us leaving Starkville, the MSU campus ministry stopped growing and started shrinking. A couple of years later, it unceremoniously closed. Our miracle building on 206 Herbert Street—one that had been dedicated to God—was sold to a family that completely renovated it and turned it into a beautiful massive home. While the mission headquarters in Florida used the proceeds to start other campus ministries in the USA, which was money well spent, I cannot ignore the fact that the lack of an intentional leadership transition plan in our small, little church was a significant leadership runway disaster.

It is painful to tell the next part of the story, but I have to in order to expose the dangers of non-existent succession planning and haphazard leadership transition.

Less than a decade after Deborah and I left Starkville for Manila, the ministry that Walter started and turned over to me had not only closed, but the building on 206 Herbert Street that God had miraculously given to us was later purchased by the Islamic Student Center. Imams renovated and transformed it into a mosque, complete with a couple of minarets.

But that's not all.

Remember Moe, the MSU student who was arrested along with Jaelyn at the Golden Triangle Regional Airport? He grew up in the house on 204 Herbert Street, right next door to our miracle-ministry house. Moe's father was the imam who led Friday night prayers for many years on 204 Herbert Street.

Once 206 Herbert Street was purchased by the Islamic Center of Mississippi, the Friday night Islamic prayer meetings were moved into the building where I used to worship, pray, and preach.[2]

LEADERSHIP TRANSITION LESSONS

Walter passed the leadership baton to me, and the church and campus ministry survived the transition. It even grew a little. Tragically, the ministry that had been entrusted to me did not survive and our miracle on Herbert Street became a mosque on Herbert Street. The building that was once a house of prayer for all nations became an Islamic prayer center.

What went wrong?

First, I had no succession plan. In my world, in those days, pastors didn't plan; they were "led by the Spirit." Second, I had no successor. Is anyone really shocked that having no succession plan often leads to having no successor? And finally, I was not involved in the leadership transition. Being 13,000 kilometers (8,600 miles) away in Manila, I had no input in the selection, training, or appointment of my successor. While I take full responsibility for my part in the Herbert Street transition failure by leaving a small but healthy church vulnerable to the consequences of a faulty leadership transition—which in turn, led to its closure—I also take a bit of comfort knowing that I am not the only spiritual leader whose inept leadership transition resulted in a runway disaster.

One of the most famous leadership transition misfires in history is recorded in the Bible. Before I summarize the story and enumerate some leadership lessons, I want to state clearly that there is much more to the story than a cautionary tale of succession planning and leadership transition failure. The primary message of the story is that God is sovereign and his plan prevails, no matter the magnitude of sin, rebellion, foolishness, or well-intended human "pilot error" that is present in this story.

Here's a quick summary of the story. After waiting for decades, Isaac and Rebekah finally had twin sons, Esau and Jacob. According to the commonly accepted succession tradition in their culture, the firstborn (Esau) was expected to be Isaac's successor.*

Scripture tells us, "When Isaac was old and his eyes were dim so that he could not see, he called Esau his older son" and thus began the leadership transition process (Genesis 27:1). Following tradition, Isaac fully intended to pass his leadership position to Esau. In doing this, however, Isaac was ignoring God's clear word that the youngest twin would lead his older brother. (See Genesis 25:23.)

Rebekah was not happy with her husband's succession plan, so she secretly crafted her own plan to install her favorite son (Jacob) as Isaac's successor.**

Rebekah's plan called for Jacob to impersonate Esau, with the goal of tricking the old, blind patriarch into accidentally blessing the younger son as his successor. Isaac seemed to fall for it and

---

* While the cultural tradition called on the eldest son to be the successor, God often defied human tradition and bypassed the elder brother. For example, God chose Isaac not Ishmael, Joseph not Reuben, and David not Eliab.

** Note to parents: If you want to ensure that your adult children hate each other and if you want to destroy your family, make sure to pick a favorite child. Works like a charm.

gave Jacob the firstborn blessing, making him the official successor. Of course, when Esau figured out that his little brother had stolen his birthright and his blessing, he vowed to kill him. Isaac was equally angry at Jacob for his duplicity. So, with the help of his mother, Jacob ran for his life.

Here are three key concepts from Isaac's story that are essential for wise succession planning and healthy leadership transition.

1. Timing

Don't wait too long to write your succession plan and implement your leadership transition. Isaac delayed his leadership transition for so long that by the time he was finally ready to relinquish his position, he was so old and blind that he installed the wrong son.*

The spiritual parallels are obvious. Some church and ministry leaders hold on until their "eyes are dim," and they no longer have clear vision or sharp discernment, which is a recipe for bad decisions. One reason my recent leadership transitions have worked so well is because I was still young and strong enough to identify mature new leaders, and to run alongside them to help when needed.

2. Unity

Get on the same page with your spouse, and with all potential successors. Isaac and Rebekah's lack of agreement was at the heart of their succession conflict. Also, the two potential successors were not in agreement. Esau wrongly assumed the traditional older brother's blessing would be his, even though he had shown contempt for tradition when he traded his birthright for a bowl of soup. Isaac should have known that Esau was undeserving of the succession blessing after he had despised his birthright; perhaps he was just too old to care. Isaac's disunity with his wife and sons

---

* Of course, looking at the story from a providential perspective, we could say that God used Isaac's blindness to cause him to bless the right son.

was his fault. In leadership transition, it is primarily the responsibility of established leaders to create and maintain unity.

3. Mission

Don't allow your own honor, ego, or legacy to get in the way of God's mission and the emerging leader. Isaac seems to have forgotten the prophetic purpose of God that was spoken to his wife on the day their twins were born. Rebekah obviously remembered it. "Two nations are in your womb, and two peoples from within you shall be divided; the one shall be stronger than the other, **the older shall serve the younger**" (Genesis 25:23). When leaders ignore the will of God or forget the mission of God, they tend to make ministry about their own honor, ego, family, or legacy. That leads to disastrous leadership transitions and deadly runway crashes. As stated in the first chapter, the remedy for most leadership transition obstacles is for the experienced leader to decrease and to sacrifice for the sake of the mission and for the empowerment of the emerging leader.

THE LEADERSHIP RUNWAY 

In almost four decades of vocational ministry, my greatest leadership failure was a catastrophic leadership transition that lamentably turned our miracle on Herbert Street into a mosque on Herbert Street. The building where MSU students once worshiped Jesus, studied the Bible, and received global mission training, became a place for Islamic prayer and Quranic study because of a succession failure.

Make no mistake about it—in a ministry context, succession planning and leadership transition matter. They matter right now, they will matter 10 years from now, and they will matter for eternity.

The rest of this book will unpack the essential elements for succession planning and leadership transition in a church and ministry context. The goal is to equip and empower leaders to build leadership runways where experienced leaders can land and emerging leaders can take off—without crashing into one another.

CHAPTER 3

Arguing for Christian Institutions

Wesley acted wisely—the souls that were awakened under his ministry he joined in class (methodical discipleship groups), and thus preserved the fruits of his labor. This I neglected, and my people are a rope of sand.

—George Whitefield, 18th Century Preacher

Other seeds fell on good soil and produced grain, some a hundredfold, some sixty, some thirty.

—Jesus, Matthew 13:8

In 1919, aviation pioneer Orville Wright advocated for "landing places" that were clearly marked and carefully designed to ensure safety during takeoff and landing. The problem for a fledgling airline industry was that creating runways would require significant initial funding as well as ongoing maintenance costs. But because safety matters, runways were funded then and continue to be funded today.

Likewise, building safe and functional "landing places" (or leadership runways) so experienced leaders can land safely and emerging ministry leaders can take off quickly is costly and will require ongoing maintenance. Just like aviation runways, leadership runways (ministry-succession plans) also require regular maintenance and costly upgrades.

Runways are usually made of flexible* pavement with an asphalt surface. For smaller planes, runways can also be made of grass, dirt, gravel, sand, salt, and even ice. I have taken off from and landed on tiny dirt runways on remote Philippine islands and on huge state-of-the-art runways in major global cities. No matter the size or material, the purpose of the runway remains the same: safe takeoff and safe landing.

Not all runways are the same, and not all succession plans or leadership transitions are the same. There are succession principles, but we do not have a one-size-fits-all succession template. The best succession plans are custom-designed for a particular leader and organization, are based on that leader's gifts and that organization's mission, and include biblical principles and best practices.

In order to build a safe runway, we must know what kind of plane will take off and land. Likewise, to build the best succession plan, we must know something about the experienced leader, the emerging leader, and the established organization or institution. The rest of this chapter will focus on ministry organizations and institutions. For some Christian leaders, the phrase "ministry

---

* "Flexible" is a key succession concept that will be covered in Chapter 10.

organization" or "ministry institution" is an oxymoron. They don't believe that Christian organizations or institutions should be built or preserved. I disagree.

In order to examine the positive impact of Christian organizations and institutions, we will go back in history to compare two highly successful ministries from the eighteenth century and two from the twentieth century. In our eighteenth-century examples—after the leadership transition from founders to next-generation leaders—one ministry experienced exponential success while the other experienced a plateau and then a slow decline. Our twentieth-century examples have the exact same results as our eighteenth-century cases—after the death of the founders, one institution endured while the other died.

In 2013, I wrote *100 Years from Now*, a book that attempted to explain and illustrate the history, mission, values, and culture of Every Nation Churches & Ministries. That book opened with a description of a large oil painting of St. Aldates Church that hangs in my Nashville office. Every day, when I walk into my office, that painting reminds me to reject superficial short-term gains and to think and build for the long haul.

Over a decade ago, while my eldest son was studying medieval history at Oxford, he attended St. Aldates—the same church John Wesley, Charles Wesley, and George Whitefield attended when they were Oxford students 300 years ago. When Deborah and I visited William in 2011, he gave us a complete city tour. For me, St. Aldates was the highlight.* The church was established over 1,000 years ago. The main part of the church building is over 900 years old (though, of course, it has had many additions and updates over the centuries).

While the old church's architecture is beautiful, its history is rich, and its membership roll is filled with world-changers, what impacted me the most was a small nondescript stone plaque listing

---

* Along with the UK's best falafel food truck parked across the street.

the names of every pastor who has ever led St. Aldates during its 1,000-year history. The list was surprisingly short. Apparently, St. Aldates' pastors live a long time and retire the day they die. As I toured other parts of this ancient church building, I couldn't get that list of pastors' names out of my mind. Even that night and the next day, I was still pondering how a local church could have so many successful leadership transitions over a 1,000-year period of time.

Every time I walk into my Nashville office, that giant painting of St. Aldates Church prompts me to pray: *God, help me learn to do succession planning and leadership transition in a way that ensures ministry continuity for decades and centuries.*

As a pastor, missionary, preacher, and leader, I try my best to think long-term, but I fear that I often get stuck in the moment and miss the long-term implications of my decisions. While reflecting on the simple stone plaque that immortalizes the name of every St. Aldates pastor, I thought about the ministry I get to lead, Every Nation Churches & Ministries. Will Every Nation still exist 1,000 years or 100 years or even 10 years after my tenure?[1] I think the answer depends, at least in part, on how well I do succession planning and leadership transition.

REVIVALS AND ROPES OF SAND

When I think about the names on that St. Aldates plaque, my mind wanders to revivals and movements throughout church history that have endured the test of time, and to many that have not. The St. Aldates pastor list reminds me that ministry success is not primarily about what happens next Sunday, next month, or next year, but what happens decades and centuries after we pass the pulpit to the next generation. Whether or not our ministry still has an impact 100 years from now has little to do with its current size, facilities, and budgets. Rather, future impact is dependent on the type of leaders we empower and the type of churches and ministries we build. My hope is that God will help us build churches and ministries that will continue to have global gospel-impact long after our leadership tenure.

Besides the names of pastors on the plaque, countless Oxford students who worshiped at St. Aldates also have had great impact on history, including three of the greatest, most influential spiritual leaders of the eighteenth century and beyond. While attending Oxford University and St. Aldates Church in the early 1700s, John and Charles Wesley, and later George Whitefield, got involved in student discipleship groups called "holy clubs." Within a few years, holy club members were mockingly called "Methodists" because of their methodical approach to discipleship.

Imagine leading a small group of college students that included John Wesley or George Whitefield, with Charles Wesley as the song leader. These three young men were dear friends and ministry colleagues. Unfortunately, due to theological, ethical, and strategic differences, Whitefield's and John Wesley's friendship was severed.*

In his biography, *Wesley the Preacher*, John Pollock described the tragedy of their relational separation and its negative impact on both of their ministries. "Together they could have done even more for Britain and America—Whitefield the incomparable preacher, Wesley the patient organizer. Instead, the evangelical revival would flow in two channels."[2]

The separation caused by their relational breakdown is the flipside of the power of unity. We will never know what was lost

---

* Wesley was obviously Wesleyan/Arminian, Whitefield was Calvinist/Reformed, thus their theological differences. Wesley was a dedicated, tireless abolitionist; Whitefield owned African slaves and even advocated for slavery in the fledgling Georgia colony. Their polar opposite views of slavery caused ethical conflict. Wesley was not just preaching, but also making disciples in small groups and building a movement within the Church of England. Whitefield was a preacher and revivalist whose ministry made an impact on hundreds of thousands on both sides of the Atlantic. This strategic difference seems to have been recognized by Whitefield towards the end of his life, producing a degree of regret.

because Wesley and Whitefield decided to "flow in two channels" rather than flowing together. Both men seem to have had moments of regret for their inability to work out their differences; and from time to time, they attempted to unite for the sake of the gospel. But ultimately, all attempts at ministry reconciliation failed. Toward the end of their lives, their friendship was restored as evidenced by Whitefield's request to have Wesley preach at his funeral, but the opportunities for ministry partnership were lost forever.

Now, we will look at their individual ministries to see what we can learn about succession planning, leadership transition, and what happens (or does not happen) when we neglect to build a leadership runway.

George Whitefield and the Great Awakening

George Whitefield is universally known as one of the greatest preachers in history. His voice can only be described as a gift from God. He once preached open air to a crowd of 80,000 people in London's Hyde Park. This was in the 1700s, so there was no electronic amplification. That's a voice designed by God for preaching.

American founding father Ben Franklin loved listening to Whitefield and calculated that 30,000 people could hear him clearly during an outdoor meeting in Philadelphia. Whitefield preached in almost every single town in England, Scotland, and Wales. He crossed the Atlantic seven times to preach in America. It is estimated that 80% of Americans heard him preach in person. Whitefield's revivals catalyzed the "Great Awakening" in the American colonies. In 34 years of preaching that included over 18,000 sermons, it is estimated that more than 10,000,000 people heard Whitefield preach. Toward the end of his life, while refusing to stop preaching even when ill, he famously said, "I would rather wear out than rust out."

According to Bishop J.C. Ryle, Whitefield:

obtained a degree of popularity such as no preacher before or since has ever reached. No preacher has ever been so universally popular in every country he visited. No preacher has ever retained his hold on his ears so entirely as he did for thirty-four years. His popularity never wanted. It was as great at the end of his days as it was at the beginning.[3]

Unfortunately, despite his popularity, as soon as Whitefield died, his ministry influence began to wane.

John Wesley and his Meticulous Methods

John Wesley was a good preacher, but not a great one like Whitefield. Riding over 250,000 miles on horseback, he preached over 42,000 sermons. His first sermon was typically preached at 5 am every day. Wesley published over 200 books, 23 full hymnals, and 5,000 tracts. He gave away almost all the money generated by his published works. At his death at 87 years old in 1791, Wesley had trained over 500 ordained preachers who were leading over 115,000 Methodist members.

Today, the World Methodist Council includes 75 million people in 76 denominations in 132 nations. There are another 600 million Pentecostals (including many Charismatics) who have Wesleyan holiness theological roots. My guess is that when the Wesley brothers were Oxford students attending holy clubs, if someone had told them that in the future they would have 75 million followers in 132 nations, they would probably think that person was crazy.

But that's what happened. Ultimately, the Whitefield revivals and the Wesleyan revivals happened because of the sovereign grace of God. They also happened because God uses faithful leaders. The reason some moves of God last and others are temporary is a mysterious combination of the sovereignty of God and the leadership of humans. On a human level, one reason the Wesley brothers are still having a global impact today is because The Methodist mission and holiness mandate was successfully passed from generation to generation, nation to nation, century to century.

Exactly how did the Wesley brothers do that? What if we could go back in time and ask George Whitefield what his friends did to make such a lasting impact? I am not sure if anyone asked that exact question, but Whitefield certainly answered it when he said, "Wesley acted wisely—the souls that were awakened under his ministry he joined in class (methodical discipleship groups), and thus preserved the fruits of his labor. This I neglected, and my people are a rope of sand."[4]

This is the great preacher talking about the great organizer, explaining that the methodical disciple-maker acted more wisely than the great preacher and revivalist. How so? Because "the souls that were awakened under his ministry" were placed in churches that had a methodical structure for discipleship and leadership development. Those structures and Christian institutions outlived the Wesley brothers.

Moments, Movements, and Institutions

Here's another way to look at it. Whitefield built moments that became a movement. If we could go back in time and attend his revival meetings, we might describe the experience as an unforgettable defining moment. As these life-altering, defining moments happened week after week, they became a revival movement that impacted cities, nations, and continents.

The Wesley brothers also created defining moments that became a movement. Their movement also became a revival that impacted cities, nations, and continents.

But here's the difference: John Wesley was not content with moments and movements. He built Christian organizations and institutions that multiplied the moments and sustained the movements. George Whitefield did not build organizations and institutions, at least none that lasted.

Perhaps the lesson from Wesley and Whitefield is that the organizations and institutions we leave behind can help regional revival moments become sustainable global movements for years, decades, and centuries.

MIRACLE MINISTRIES AND HEALING EVANGELISTS

Another more recent comparative study of leadership transitions involves the evangelists Kathryn Kuhlman and Aimee Semple McPherson.

In his book *The Century of the Holy Spirit,* historian Vinson Synan describes the Pentecostal and charismatic revivals as "the most important religious movement of the entire twentieth century."[5] From the beginning of the Pentecostal movement on January 1, 1901, in Topeka, Kansas, until today, the gifts of the Spirit have been front and center, including the power gifts of healing and miracles. Two of the most prominent and controversial healing evangelists of the twentieth century were Aimee Semple McPherson and Kathryn Kuhlman. Like Wesley and Whitefield, they both had world-changing ministries. Unfortunately, similar to Wesley and Whitefield, the ministry of one continues to impact millions around the world while the other is a modern day "rope of sand."

Kathryn Kuhlman (1907-1976)

By the age of 16, equipped with a 10th-grade education, Kathryn Kuhlman launched into full-time evangelistic ministry. By the age of 28, she had built the 2,000-seat Denver Revival Tabernacle. Let's pause and let that fact sink in for a moment. A barely educated female* preacher built and filled a 2,000-seat church building by the age of 28. Wow!

---

*Remember, this was the 1930s when women did not typically have the opportunity to preach or lead. In light of this cultural norm, the fact that she, as a young, single woman, achieved this level of influence is noteworthy.

Unfortunately, Kuhlman would be the subject of multiple controversies over the next few decades of ministry. Not long after the ribbon-cutting, she married an evangelist, who divorced his wife to marry her. According to Synan, "This destroyed her Denver Ministry." About six years later, she left her husband, moved to the other side of the USA, and started over near Pittsburgh. It was during this time that Kuhlman first started seeing miracle healings in her evangelistic meetings. By the mid-1960s, the miracles continued, and she relocated to Los Angeles where she consistently filled the 7,000-seat Shrine Auditorium for the next 10 years.[6]

Eventually, Kuhlman conducted healing crusades all over the world, with her global ministry lasting over 40 years. Because of radio, television, and constant travel, between 1940 and 1970, she was one of the most well-known preachers in the world. Over two-million people self-reported being healed in her meetings.

She died in 1976. While the Kathryn Kuhlman Foundation continued in diminishing capacity for another forty years, by 1982, its nationwide radio broadcasting was terminated due to lack of funding. By 2016, the ministry foundation bearing her name no longer existed.

Aimee Semple McPherson (1890-1944)

Aimee Semple McPherson founded one of the first megachurches in America, Angelus Temple in Los Angeles.

In the 1920s, McPherson's name appeared on the front pages of major American newspapers an average of three times a week. Her funeral in 1944 drew more than 50,000 people. Like Kuhlman, her preaching and healing ministry attracted thousands and impacted millions. Also, like Kuhlman, she had multiple failed marriages, along with rumors of infidelity. As her ministry grew, accusations of financial mismanagement followed her. Perhaps because of her reputation as a healing evangelist with hundreds of documented miracles, these scandals did not seem to negatively impact the crowds that continued to flock to her meetings in desperate need of a miracle.

Her most infamous scandal was her "kidnapping" and escape, which captured the attention of national press and led to a court case accusing her of fraud. Eventually the case was dropped, but the accusations never disappeared. Despite the scandals, the institution she founded outlived her and continues to grow all over the world.

McPherson organized her ministry, not into small discipleship groups like Wesley, but into local churches that joined together to form a Pentecostal denomination—the International Church of the Foursquare Gospel. Today, Foursquare includes 88,000 ordained ministers serving 9 million church members and 90,000 churches in 144 nations. In 2016, Foursquare reported over 2.5 million baptisms globally. Think about that: 2.5 million baptisms in one year!

While Kuhlman and McPherson both saw thousands of miraculous healings and genuine salvations in their meetings and both ended with multiple scandals, there is one major difference in the fruitfulness and endurance of their ministries after they died: organizations and institutions. In the end, Kathryn Kuhlman created a healing movement that did not endure. Aimee Semple McPherson created a Pentecostal movement that has been sustained by Christian organizations and institutions including the Foursquare* denomination, Christian radio stations, Life Pacific University, and multiple leadership training institutions and publishing ventures.

GOD DOES NOT NEED INSTITUTIONS, BUT...

Humans have a relatively short lifespan. Institutions don't. While some institutions die young, and many more start dying at their

---

* If you're interested in reading more about the Foursquare Movement, check out "The Vine and the Branches: A History of the Foursquare Movement," by Nathaniel Van Cleeve.

founder's funeral, technically an institution can live for centuries, even millennia. For this reason, it is not surprising that healthy Christian institutions sometimes have a greater gospel impact after their founders are dead and buried than when they were alive and leading.

After making the case for Christian organizations and institutions in the context of succession planning and leadership transitions, I feel compelled to end this chapter with a disclaimer lest anyone trust in organizations and institutions rather than in God. Let me be clear: God does not need human institutions to accomplish his divine purpose, but he often chooses to use human institutions.*

In *Art and Faith: A Theology of Making*, Makoto Fujimura names the necessary starting point and divine motive if an institution is to be "useful to society" long after the founders are forgotten.

> There's a type of need to justify the existence of the institution of the church (or any nonprofit organization) to be "useful to society" and therefore useful to God. While the impetus is noble, we must start from the correct biblical understanding of God's self-sufficiency. God does not need any of our institutions to exist, period.[7]

If God does not need human institutions, then why build them? The answer, according to Fujimura, is because "God's exuberant love invites us, broken vessels of God's choosing, to co-create the New Creation through Christ."[8]

Christian institutions exist, not because God needs human or institutional help, but because God wants to partner with humans to "co-create." Like so much of life, it's about a relationship with God.

---

* For more on Christian institutions that continue to minister long after their founders' deaths, see Appendix A: "The Lasting Power of Christian Institutions."

THE LEADERSHIP RUNWAY 

Just as Orville Wright called for "landing places" that were clearly marked for takeoff and landing, this book is a call to build leadership runways so experienced leaders can land safely and emerging leaders can gain elevation quickly.

If we are okay with a church or ministry dying with its founder (or becoming a mosque), then there is no need for succession planning and no need for this book.

However, if we want to create and maintain a safe place for established leaders to land and emerging leaders to take off, and if we want to build organizations and institutions that outlive their founders, then we will need to build leadership pipelines and leadership runways.*

---

* Leadership pipelines is a concept introduced by Ram Charan, Stephan Drotter, et al. in their book entitled, *The Leadership Pipeline: How to Build the Leadership-Powered Company.*

Prepare Emerging Leaders to Lead the Organization

The leadership runway succession strategy depends on identifying potential leaders, developing future leaders, and empowering emerging leaders. No matter how good the succession plan, without a healthy leadership pipeline, every leadership transition is doomed.

Throughout Part II, David will serve as our example of how God prepares emerging leaders for greater leadership positions. In the beginning, David had no idea that God was using his mundane life as a shepherd boy to lay the foundation for his future leadership roles. For ministry leaders, spiritual formation and leadership development are always happening, but we rarely realize or appreciate how or why they are happening. We trudge through our less-than-spectacular daily routines, while waiting for our big spiritual moment, not realizing that the mundane routine is exactly how God prepares the hearts of leaders for greater things.

In a ministry context, as we consider possible successors, we are looking for sanctified hearts, skilled hands, spiritual habits, and ultimately sacred callings. In *No Man Is an Island,* Thomas Merton makes the heart/hands/habits connection, albeit with different vocabulary. "My soul does not find itself unless it acts. Therefore, it must act. Stagnation and inactivity bring spiritual death."[1] These action-oriented words are unexpected from a revered mystic. But when the world's most famous Trappist monk writes about the necessity of connecting the soul with action (i.e. connecting the heart with hands and habits) and about the spiritual danger of inactivity, that's a good time to take heed.

Like Merton, Professor James K. A. Smith connects heart formation with habit-forming practices. In *Desiring the Kingdom,* Smith writes, "the mall and its 'parachurch' extensions in television and advertising offer a daily liturgy for the formation of the heart."[2]

Knowing that the culture is working on our hearts, Smith makes a compelling case for what the church must do to form people who "desire the kingdom." He explains that individuals are formed by their habits, whether those habits are centered around shopping, watching television, and scrolling social media or around worship and the word of God.

Too often we are not even aware when or how God is doing deep work in our hearts as we go about our daily routines. David was busy with the mundane task of tending his father's sheep—same boring routine day after day after day. On a couple of occasions, the boredom was interrupted by a lion or a bear. Years later, David realized that these seemingly random encounters with deadly predators prepared him to face the ultimate predator, Goliath.

As always, when talking about leadership, we will start with the heart, specifically the "sanctified heart."

CHAPTER 4

Protecting Sanctified Hearts

Spiritual formation is a process of being conformed to the image of Christ for the sake of others.

—M. Robert Mulholland Jr.

With upright heart he shepherded them.

—Asaph, Psalm 78:72

Wax on, wax off. Breathe in through nose, out of mouth. Wax on, wax off. Don't forget to breathe, very important."

With this strange instruction, Daniel LaRusso's first and most important karate lesson began. Of course, young Daniel-san had no idea that washing and waxing Mr. Miyagi's impressive fleet of antique cars was actually preparing him to fight Johnny Lawrence in the 1984 All-Valley Under 18 Karate Championship. *The Karate Kid* movie is like a 20th-century leadership parable, with Mr. Miyagi throwing down wisdom in every scene.

The classic "wax on, wax off" metaphor contains three leadership preparation and heart formation principles: mundane, mentoring, and mastery.

1. Mundane

The heart formation part of leadership preparation is often mundane and repetitive—like washing and waxing cars, painting fences, and sanding floors. For those aspiring to greater spiritual leadership rather than karate championships, preparation might include the mundane routine of daily Bible reading, devotional prayer, seasonal fasting, and private serving. Quite often, heart formation is so mundane that we are not even aware that something extraordinarily transformative is happening. But eventually, mundane repetition pays off spectacularly. When evaluating emerging leaders as possible successors, look for leaders who willingly embrace the mundane, not just those enamored with the spectacular.

2. Mentoring

For emerging spiritual leaders, heart formation also requires mentoring, and mentoring requires living, human mentors. The spiritual leader who names only dead people like Augustine, Luther, Calvin, or Wesley as mentors is not only missing the point of mentoring, but also the power of embodied relationships. Mr. Miyagi chuckled and rolled his eyes when he commented on Daniel-san's attempt to learn karate from a book rather than from a *sensei*. I'm obviously not anti-book. I write and read books. Books are a good start, but time with human mentors—typically older and more experienced—is required for every emerging leader who wants to grow deeper, wiser, and stronger. If potential leaders are unwilling to be mentored by experienced leaders, they probably should not be part of your succession plan.

3. Mastery

Heart formation and leadership preparation happens as we focus on the mastery of the basics, before moving on to advanced skills.* Martial arts legend Bruce Lee recognized the power of mastery when he said, "I fear not the man who has practiced 10,000 kicks, but I do fear the man who has practiced one kick 10,000 times." Practicing one kick 10,000 times is certainly a step towards mastery. Though Malcolm Gladwell's "10,000 Hour Rule," popularized in his book *Outliers*, has come under a bit of scrutiny and criticism of late (for underemphasizing the role of a mentor), I think that if taken as a principle rather than a literal 10,000 hours and with the presence of a mentor, the principle stands. What if we apply the 10,000 hour principle and the power of repetition to heart formation? Imagine the leadership formation when a leader consistently reads the Bible 10,000 days—that's 27 years of Bible reading! Or imagine the heart transformation when a leader consistently starts every year with a week of prayer, fasting, and consecration for 5, 10, 20 consecutive years.

THE HEART OF LEADERSHIP

Before we look at the formation of David's heart, as King Saul's divinely designated successor, we need a simple definition of the word "sanctified." The most basic meaning of sanctified—to set apart or consecrate as holy—has two distinct perspectives. The

---

*Like the "crane kick!"

divine perspective tells us that God sovereignly sets a person or thing apart for his purpose. The human perspective requires people to respond to God by consecrating themselves for his purpose.

Like Daniel,* David's lifelong heart formation and leadership development started with a three-part foundation: the mundane life of a shepherd, mentoring by Samuel and Nathan, and the mastery of specific skills. In each phase, from youth to old age, David's heart was the central issue.

David's Heart at the Start

From the start, David's leadership calling was about the heart. You know the story. God decided it was time for a leadership transition from King Saul, so he sent his prophet Samuel to Bethlehem to pick one of Jesse's sons to be Saul's successor. As soon as Samuel laid eyes on David's oldest brother, Eliab, he said, "Surely the Lord's anointed!" God corrected his easily-impressed prophet, "Do not look on his appearance or on the height of his stature, because I have rejected him. For the Lord sees not as man sees: man looks on the outward appearance, but **the Lord looks on the heart.**"

One by one, seven of Jesse's sons impressed the prophet by their outward appearance, and seven times God said, "Nope, not that one." Finally Jesse called his youngest and least-impressive son from the farm and instantly, the prophet said, "That's the one!" This time, he was correct and "the Spirit of the Lord rested upon David from that day forward" (See 1 Samuel 16:1-13).

From the start, David was called by God and chosen by Samuel as Saul's successor—not because of outward appearance but because of his heart.

David's Heart at Halftime

David started with a good heart, but by halftime, he had self-inflicted heart disease. We are not told exactly what corrupted

---

* I'm referring to Daniel the Karate Kid, not the lion-tamer.

David's heart—maybe the usual suspects: fame, riches, power—but we know what happened. David's adultery and abuse of authority turned his clean hands and pure heart into bloody hands and a hard heart. Because God always pursues us, even when we are running from him, he sent a prophet-mentor named Nathan to speak truth to power. David received the prophetic rebuke and cried out to God, not for the protection of his reputation, wealth, or position, but for the restoration of his once pure heart.

Remembering that his original leadership appointment was not because he was a natural-born leader, but because "the Lord looks on the heart," David's halftime prayer focused on his own heart. "Create in me a **clean heart**, O God, and renew a right spirit within me" (Psalm 51:10). God answered David's prayer and cleaned up his heart.

David's Heart at the Finish Line

Through all of his ups and downs, David's heart was the central issue at the start and in the middle of his leadership career, but what about as he approached his finish line? Was his heart still his central concern? Let's jump ahead to the end of David's story as he was in the final stages of his succession plan to install Solomon as the new king. His prayer indicates that an "upright heart" is still the core focus for spiritual leadership. "I know, my God, that **you test the heart** and have pleasure in **uprightness**. In the **uprightness of my heart** I have freely offered all these things" (1 Chronicles 29:17).

There was something about young David's heart that landed him on Samuel's succession-plan shortlist to replace King Saul. Somewhere on the journey, his heart went astray, causing a deadly runway crash. When confronted with hard truth by a mentor, David humbly and sincerely repented and cried out to God to cleanse his dirty heart. God answered.

At the end of his life, David's primary prayer concern was still his own heart, but now he was also concerned with the heart of his successor.

David's Prayer for His Successor's Heart

Knowing that God requires "clean hands and a pure heart" for everyone who would serve him, David prayed that God would "keep forever such purposes and thoughts **in the hearts of your people** and direct **their hearts toward you**." After praying for the people, David turned his prayer to his successor. "Grant to Solomon my son **a whole heart** that he may keep your commandments, your testimonies, and your statutes" (1 Chronicles 29:18-19).

From David's original calling to his prayer for his successor, the heart was the main concern. As we identify and develop leaders and potential successors, skilled hands and spiritual habits are important, but the heart is always the most important issue. May God grant every future church and ministry leader "a whole heart" to discern and pursue God's purpose with uprightness and integrity.

THE LORD TESTS THE HEART

In 2008, my wife, Deborah, and our three sons were standing in a long line with about 100 other tourists who had signed up for the basic White House tour. Just before we got to what I thought was a standard airport-type metal detector, two large heavily armed muscular men with dark shades appeared on my right and left and politely but sternly asked me to follow them. It was immediately obvious to me that they were not really asking me to follow them. I had no choice. They interrogated me in a side room, specifically asking if I had recently had contact with radioactive nuclear material.

I smiled and confirmed that, yes, I had recently been in contact with radioactive nuclear material, in fact it was inside my heart. They smiled for the first time and said, "That's what we suspected." Then they pointed to the door and said, "Enjoy your White House tour."

Five days prior, while driving home from preaching a Sunday night church service, I experienced chest pains, complete with pain shooting through my arm, and sweat pouring from my forehead. I sat in my car through a couple of green to yellow to red light cycles, then I felt completely normal and drove home. As I crawled into bed, I casually mentioned this experience to Deborah, who demanded I get out of bed and into the car, right now.

She drove me to St. Thomas Heart Center in West Nashville, like a Formula 1 driver, where I was rushed into a diagnosis room and drilled with rapid-fire questions. My answers led to a nuclear stress test, where they injected a small amount of radioactive material into my heart so they could get a clear picture of what was going on.

The good news is that I passed two days of multiple heart tests with flying colors. Upon further questioning, the doctors determined that my chest pain was probably due to a wakeboarding accident that happened the day before, which caused a pulled pectoral muscle and possibly a temporary dislocation of some sort. They sent me home with some pain meds (and a bill the size of a home mortgage).

Less than a week later, what I thought was a White House routine metal detector included a device that could pick up and pinpoint the location of minor traces of radioactive materials a quarter of a mile away. The two security officers said they had been watching me for fifteen minutes as I waited in line, because their machine detected that tiny trace of radioactive residue in my heart.

For those trained and equipped to notice, the fact that I had endured and passed a heart test was obvious. Likewise, as established leaders consider emerging leaders in the leadership runway succession strategy, we are looking for leaders whose hearts have been tested, formed, and transformed by God. If they have had divine heart tests, there might not be traces of radiation, but there will be a fire burning for him.

Clean Hands and Pure Hearts

Every spiritual leader has felt at times (maybe all the time) that they are in the deep end, way over their heads, with no clue what to do next—the feeling that the task at hand is beyond their training, ability, knowledge, and budget. They know they need to get in God's presence and hear his voice. There is no human solution; only divine intervention and direction will save the day. David gave words to that quintessential leadership conundrum, and more importantly he gave an answer.

Here's the question: "Who can ascend the hill of the Lord and who can stand in his holy place?" David's answer: The person who has "clean hands and a **pure heart**" (Psalm 24:3-4).

Jesus said essentially the same thing in the Sermon on the Mount. "Blessed are the **pure in heart**, for they shall see God" (Matthew 5:8). Okay, so a pure heart is necessary, but where do I get one of those? How are impurities removed from the heart? And, how does a leader maintain pure heart motives?

As with all important questions about high-level spiritual leadership, the Bible has the answer. "The crucible is for silver, and the furnace is for gold, and **the Lord tests hearts**" (Proverbs 17:3). A crucible is literally a ceramic or metal container used to melt metals at extremely high temperatures. Metaphorically, a crucible is a severe test or situation of extreme pressure that changes a person. When silver is put in a crucible and the heat is turned up, the impurities and contaminants are exposed. Same with our hearts. When God puts us through the fire and pressure, he is not punishing us. Rather, he is testing our hearts and exposing the impurities and contaminants.

Throughout Scripture, we often find God testing his leaders before promoting them to the next level of leadership. These tests have nothing to do with physical strength or mental acuity, although new leadership levels often demand increased physical endurance and mental prowess. God's tests are primarily heart tests.

Question: How does God test the heart? Answer: Through pressure, heat, and fire.

God Tested Abraham

One of the most terrifying stories in the Bible starts with this phrase: "God tested Abraham." This test had nothing to do with Abraham's devotional disciplines, religious routines, or theological acumen. It was a heart test. Like all heart tests, this one was designed to expose a potential idol in Abraham's heart. And like many heart tests, it was painful and seemed unfair.

God said to Abraham, "Take your son, your only son Isaac, whom you love, and go to the land of Moriah, and offer him there as a burnt offering."* I don't know what I would have done had I been in Abraham's situation and God told me to sacrifice my son. God didn't tell Abraham, "Don't worry, this is just a test." As far as Abraham knew, this was a straightforward command to kill his son. It made no sense, but God had spoken and Abraham did his best to obey. Of course, as we read the story, we know right from verse 1 that it is a test, and we know the outcome. However, in real time, like Abraham and Daniel-san we are not aware that we are being tested and prepared for greatness.

Knowing that heart tests involve fire, heat, pressure, and sacrifice, my tendency is to avoid them whenever possible. Not David. Testing of the heart was so core to David's understanding of God that when he prayed, he referred to God as "you who test the hearts" (Psalm 7:9), and actually prayed for God to test him: "Prove me, O Lord, and try me; test my heart" (Psalm 26:2). Perhaps we should pause a minute or two and pray that brave prayer right now. ***Test my heart, O Lord!***

---

*See Genesis 22 for the full story.

THE LEADERSHIP RUNWAY 

The Leadership Runway succession strategy requires healthy leaders at all levels of the church and ministry. What good is a state-of-the-art runway and a fleet of new jets without skilled pilots?

As we consider leaders for promotion, we are not necessarily looking for charismatic personalities, academic achievements, or natural-born leaders. Rather, we are primarily looking for upright and sanctified hearts. For potential successors, a good heart is a good start, but without skillful hands, spiritual habits, and a sacred calling the succession plan (and the new leader) will fail.

To be considered for a leadership position in a church and ministry context, the emerging leader must be someone who spends time in the presence of the Lord. David wrote that standing in the presence of a holy God required "clean hands and a pure heart." A quick look at David's many failures tells us that dirty hands can be cleansed and impure hearts can be purified, so this is not about perfection, but direction. Is the potential leader heading in the right direction in terms of a relationship with the Lord? The psalmist Asaph summarized David's leadership with the same two words that David used: heart and hand. "With an **upright heart** he shepherded them and guided them with his **skillful hand**" (Psalm 78:72).

We end this chapter on the heart of leadership with David's prayer about his own heart, after a grievous failure. "Create in me a clean heart, O God, and renew a right spirit within me" (Psalm 51:10). Amen.

Promoting Skilled Hands

I don't even have any good skills. You know, like nunchuck skills, bow hunting skills, computer hacking skills. Girls only want boyfriends who have great skills!

—Napoleon Dynamite

David prevailed over the Philistine with a sling and with a stone.

—Prophet Samuel, 1 Samuel 17:50

It was the summer of 2004, and I was sitting in the bleachers enduring Tennessee's torturous heat and humidity, watching my 16-year-old son crush multiple inside-out forehand winners. This was one of his better tournaments that summer. Every shot in his arsenal was working, especially that lethal forehand.

As soon as the match ended, the dad of his opponent extended his right hand and said, "Congratulations." As our brief handshake concluded, he smiled and spoke truth that only a tennis dad could appreciate: "I bet you paid a lot of money for that forehand."

All tennis parents and coaches understand that statement. Let me explain it to everyone else. Tennis is not primarily an athletic sport. Like golf, tennis is a skill sport with a strong mental component. That means a non-athletic player with advanced skills will always beat a more athletic player with average skills. Athleticism only matters when the two players have equal skills. Then the better athlete usually wins (provided there is no mental meltdown). That also means for every teenager with advanced tennis skills, there is a parent who paid a lot of money to a lot of coaches to develop said skills. Yes, as the tennis dad stated, I definitely "paid a lot of money for that forehand" and for that backhand, and serve, but not so much the volleys. Plus, my son put in countless hours of work and buckets of sweat. Fortunately, I recovered much of my investment when he and his two brothers earned NCAA Division 1 tennis scholarships. Their hard work, plus the money paid to coaches, resulted in high-level tennis skills.

I believe skill acquisition always pays off, especially when we are building leadership skills.

THE SURPRISING POWER OF SHEPHERD SKILLS

What do *Rocky, Rudy, Hoosiers, Invictus,* and *Slumdog Millionaire* have in common? They are all popular movies that feature "David

v. Goliath" stories where the underdog beats the odds and gets the girl or the gold. No matter the nation or culture, people all over the world love a good underdog story.

Would it surprise you to know that in the original David versus Goliath story, some people think Goliath was actually the underdog? It certainly surprised me. In a fight to the death, how could a huge experienced warrior be considered an underdog when pitted against a shepherd boy with no military experience?

Malcolm Gladwell's best-selling book, *David and Goliath: Underdogs, Misfits, and the Art of Battling Giants* makes the case that David defeating Goliath was not a surprise, and that all bets should have been on David for the win. Despite his inferior strength and diminutive size, David won because of his skill with the shepherd sling. According to Gladwell, "Slinging took an extraordinary amount of skill and practice. But in experienced hands, the sling was a devastating weapon. Paintings from medieval times show slingers hitting birds in midflight. Irish slingers were said to be able to hit a coin from as far away as they could see it, and in the Old Testament Book of Judges, slingers are described as being accurate within a 'hair's breadth.'"[1]

Israeli Defense Forces ballistics expert Eitan Hirsch calculated that a projectile, like the river stone David hand-picked for Goliath, when slung by a skilled slinger could have hit Goliath's head "with a velocity of thirty-four meters per second—more than enough to penetrate his skull and render him unconscious, or dead. In terms of stopping power, that is equivalent to a modern-fair-sized handgun."[2]

Scripture tells us that on the day of the battle, "David rose early in the morning and left the sheep with a keeper and took the provisions and went, as Jesse had commanded him." David was not a soldier. He was a shepherd. The only reason he was anywhere near the battlefield is because his father had told him to leave the sheep and deliver some food to his brothers who were frontline soldiers.

After completing his task, David was supposed to immediately return to his shepherding duties. But he got distracted—by the call of God (See 1 Samuel 17).

As David assessed the situation, his confidence rose. As he remembered his battles as a shepherd, he knew he had the skills to take down the giant. Trying to convince King Saul to allow him to fight Goliath one-on-one, David explained, "Your servant used to keep sheep for his father. And when there came a lion, or a bear, and took a lamb from the flock, I went after him and struck him and delivered it out of his mouth. And if he arose against me, I caught him by his beard and struck him and killed him. Your servant has struck down both lions and bears, and this uncircumcised Philistine shall be like one of them, for he has defied the armies of the living God" (1 Samuel 17). David had fought "lions and bears" and lived to tell about it. Not one lion and one bear. Both words are plural, meaning multiple lions and multiple bears.

After David had convinced King Saul to allow him to fight the giant, Saul tried to convince David to use his high-tech military weaponry and armor, similar to Goliath's. David tried it on, but declined "for he had not tested them." In other words, David knew he did not have the skills necessary to properly use the king's weapons, and he had no time to learn new sword skills. He explained to King Saul, "I cannot go with these, for I have not tested them." While the professional soldiers were wondering how this crazy shepherd boy without a sword, spear, or armor could possibly fight a giant armed warrior, David quietly picked up his shepherd staff and then "chose five smooth stones from the brook and put them in his shepherd's pouch. His sling was in his hand, and he approached the Philistine." David was uncomfortable and insecure in Saul's armor, but comfortable and confident with the shepherd's staff, stones, and sling. He was unsure how to fight with armor and sword, but he knew exactly what to do with a leather sling and river stones. He had put in his 10,000 hours slinging stones to protect his sheep.

Here's what happened. "When the Philistine arose and came and drew near to meet David, David ran quickly toward the battle line to meet the Philistine. And David put his hand in his bag and took out a stone and slung it and struck the Philistine on his forehead. The stone sank into his forehead, and he fell on his face to the ground. So David prevailed over the Philistine with a sling and with a stone, and struck the Philistine and killed him. There was no sword in the hand of David. Then David ran and stood over the Philistine and took his sword and drew it out of its sheath and killed him and cut off his head with it."

Whether you accept that Goliath was the underdog or not, humanly speaking, there is one reason David won. It was not his superior battle gear or physical strength. It was his skill with the sling, a skill common to all shepherds in his day. The psalmist Asaph connected David's shepherd skills with his future leadership roles: "With upright heart he shepherded them and guided them with his skillful hand" (Psalm 78:72).

In the previous chapter, we discussed David's upright and sanctified heart. This chapter focuses on David's skillful hands.

THREE SKILLS FOR MINISTRY LEADERS

Olympic sprint champion Usain Bolt explains the importance of adding skill to natural talent: "Talent you have naturally. Skill is only developed by hours and hours of work." Of course, Bolt was born with natural running talent. Everyone is born with some talent, but many never put in the hard work to develop the right skills to maximize their talent. Bolt became the fastest human on earth because he added skills to his natural talent through hours of hard work over many years. Similarly, basketball legend Larry Bird explains, "A winner is someone who recognizes his God-given talents, works his tail off to develop them into skills, and uses these skills to accomplish his goals." There's that formula again: talent plus work produces skills.

The Leadership Runway strategy recognizes that skill development must be added to natural talent and divine calling in order to lead at the highest level. Depending on the position and leadership responsibilities, many different leadership skills might be required, but three skills are essential for all spiritual leaders no matter the position: vision casting, critical thinking, and culture building. If any one of these are missing or deficient, then we can expect a leadership runway disaster.

1. Vision Casting Skills

The Leadership Runway succession strategy requires leaders who understand the importance of vision. As the plane is landing on the runway, the established leader must continually clarify and cast a compelling vision at all levels of the organization. Also, a mentor team should be helping all emerging leaders deeply understand the vision and upgrade their vision casting skills.

All leaders are vision casters. The senior leader is the chief vision caster. Notice I said vision caster, not vision crafter or vision creator. Founders are typically vision crafters. All leaders who come after the founders inherit a vision that has already been crafted. The new leader's job is to run with the vision, not to change it or craft a new one. Here's an important question when interviewing potential leaders in the leadership runway succession strategy: Is this potential leader willing to cast the vision that someone else crafted and resist the temptation to create a new vision?

What is a vision and what is vision casting? To answer that question, let's look at a story in the Old Testament. In the years leading up to the Babylonian captivity, it was a dark time in Jerusalem. God seemed distant and deaf. The first two chapters of Habakkuk record prophetic complaints to God about the rampant injustice in his culture. "Justice never goes forth" but when it does, "justice goes forth perverted" (Habakkuk 1:1-4). Chapter 2 records God's answer to Habakkuk's prophetic complaint. "Write the vision; make it plain on tablets, so he may run who reads it. For still the vision awaits its appointed time; it hastens to the end—it will not lie. If it seems slow, wait for it; it will surely come; it will not delay" (Habakkuk 2:2-3). God's answer to his leader during difficult times was to "write the vision and make it plain." In other words, be a vision caster.

Notice what God told Habakkuk about vision casting. First, the vision must be written. Otherwise, it will be forgotten instantly and edited frequently. Second, it must be plain. We've all seen vision statements that are convoluted and confusing. After reading and rereading, we still have no idea what they mean. Third, those who hear the vision are supposed to run with it. That means they are expected to own it, live it, pray for it, sacrifice for it, and be empowered to preach it, post it, podcast it, and propagate it every way possible. Finally, and this one is difficult for visionary leaders, but God exhorted Habakkuk to be patient. When the vision seems slow (to visionaries, it always seems slow): "Wait for it. It will surely come; it will not delay."

It is the job of experienced leaders to help emerging leaders upgrade their vision casting skills. When leaders cast vision, they are extending an invitation to mission, a call to participate in God's story, and a challenge to sacrifice for said vision. Let's talk about these three concepts briefly.

Vision casting is an invitation to join a community on mission, not to do mission alone. As top leaders cast vision, it is vital that we present it as an invitation, not as an obligation. There is no room for a leader who uses guilt, shame, coercion, or manipulation. As we make the invitation to mission, remember that the vision does not belong to the leader alone, but to the whole team. Jesus invited the original twelve to community and mission. If they wanted to be on mission with Jesus, they had to be on mission together.

Vision casting is a call to participate in God's story. Vision casting is best done through storytelling, not through statistics, strategies, or mission statements. Data engages (or disengages) the mind. Story engages and moves the heart. The most successful modern newscasters don't just report the facts, they tell the stories. Likewise, the best vision casters aren't just truth-tellers, they are primarily storytellers. As visionary leaders tell God's story, people will volunteer to live and spread that story.

Vision casting is a challenge to sacrifice for a cause beyond self. The most compelling vision casting unapologetically presents a challenge to sacrifice. The bigger the vision, the greater the sacrifice. Great vision casters never hesitate to call for sacrifice. Jesus expected his followers to pick up their crosses, crucify self, and follow, no matter the cost. And they did. Following the example of Jesus, 16th-century missionary Francis Xavier challenged students to "give up their small ambitions and come eastward to preach the gospel of Christ." Because Xavier was not afraid to call believers to sacrifice, thousands sacrificed everything to join God's mission in India and Japan. As we consider potential successors at the highest leadership levels in our churches and ministry organizations, they must be willing to sacrifice and to call others to sacrifice for the sake of the gospel. Sacrifice is the heart of great vision casting.

2. Critical Thinking Skills

In our cut-and-paste copycat world, critical-thinking skills are as elusive as Bigfoot and the Loch Ness Monster. That might be because it has never been easier to simply copy whatever the celebrity leaders are saying. If they have a famous ministry and a huge social media following, we wrongly assume that they must be doing something right, so we mindlessly copy rather than think.

In 2013, over 200 Every Nation leaders were gathered in Bali, Indonesia, to upgrade leadership skills. The highlight of our gathering was Filipino pastor Jon Naron's description of a leader's job. Jon asked, "What do leaders do?" His answer was simple, profound, and practical: "Leaders think, meet, and do." According to Jon, the starting point for doing is thinking, then meeting with others to clarify those thoughts. Once we think and meet, then we do. Most leaders have been tormented by long unproductive meetings. This is what happens when we do a meeting without first investing sufficient time thinking. When leaders take time to think deeply before meeting, the meetings are usually shorter and more productive. Other leaders think, then go straight to action without ever meeting with others to refine the ideas. This is also unproductive. Then there are the "ready, fire, aim" leaders who don't waste time thinking or meeting, they just do. What they do rarely lasts, but they stay busy. Jon's way (and order) is better. Think. Meet. Do.

But doesn't everyone think all the time? Yes, and many of those thoughts are less than profound and the opposite of wise, so we are not just talking about brain activity, but critical thinking. Because our thoughts are a constant mixture of truth and distortion, discernment and confusion, faith and fear, love and selfishness, hope and despair—spiritual leaders must develop the basic skills of critical thinking.

In the context of the leadership runway succession strategy, what are the critical thinking skills we are looking for as we consider a potential successor?

Here are seven components of critical thinking and seven questions that might help jump-start critical thinking when facing a problem or situation:

Observation: What are the details? Be aware. Be intentional. Be observant. Take notes. Focus on the big picture, then on the specifics. Repeat. Big picture. Tiny details. Ponder the history and context before proposing solutions. Observe and record details. Observe and record details. Observe and record details.

Reflection: What am I missing? While observation looks outward, reflection looks inward. Reflection acknowledges that I don't know everything, that I'm probably missing something. Critical thinking forces leaders to willingly—and regularly—face their limitations, to take a humble posture. Those who already know everything and never make mistakes have no need for reflection, and thus are unable to do critical thinking.

Interpretation: What does it mean? Observation and reflection usually yield abundant information. Piles of uninterpreted information are rarely helpful, sometimes detrimental. Once gathered, the details must be understood and the information must be interpreted. Because interpretation requires a deep understanding of context, I recommend developing cross-cultural skills and gathering multi-cultural, multi-generational teams when doing critical thinking.

Discernment: What is God's perspective? The situation has been observed, the date reflected upon, and the details interpreted. This is a good start. But it's not enough in a ministry organization. God alone knows his plans, purposes, and timing for you and your ministry. While the facts might point in one direction, God's perspective often leads in a different one. Remember, David was not the obvious pick to replace King Saul. Discernment looks for God's perspective.

Contextualization: What are the sociocultural implications? Data in a vacuum divorced from cultural context usually leads to wrong conclusions, false assumptions, and bad decisions, thus the need to contextualize. What is helpful in one place might be destructive elsewhere.

Application: What should we do about it? Contextualization should lead to application, but if application precedes contextualization, we usually cause more problems than we solve. All the hard work done up to this point—observation, reflection, interpretation, discernment, contextualization—is for the sole purpose of application. Important warning: application does not necessarily mean action. The answer to the question of what we should do about it might be to do nothing, or to wait. Sometimes the application step calls for maintaining the status quo, sometimes for gradual action, sometimes for urgent action.

Action: What is the next step? The prep work has been done. The application calls for action. God has given a green light. You began this process with a need or an expectation. It would be easy to jump to this final question and get on with it, but the critical thinker endures the whole process for the best result.

These seven concepts and questions are designed to empower critical thinking, resulting in a leader who is an effective decision-maker and problem-solver.

3. Culture Building Skills

This leadership skill is so vital in *The Leadership Runway* that all of Chapter 8 addresses it.

THE LEADERSHIP RUNWAY 

For a pilot to safely land a jet on a runway, skilled hands are required. Similarly, for an experienced leader to make a successful leadership transition to an emerging leader, skilled hands are also required. But in the ministry world, an upright heart must accompany skilled hands. The two-fold description of David's leadership in Psalm 78 is the baseline for established and emerging leaders if the leadership runway succession strategy is to succeed.

"With **upright heart** he shepherded them and guided them with his **skillful hand**." But, that's not all. For long-term sustainability at the highest ministry leadership levels, spiritual habits are non-negotiable.

76

"With **upright heart** he shepherded them and guided them with his **skillful hand**." But, that's not all. For long-term sustainability at the highest ministry leadership levels, spiritual habits are non-negotiable.

CHAPTER 6

Pursuing Spiritual Habits

The chains of habit are generally too small to be felt until they are too strong to be broken.

—Samuel Johnson

Three times a day he got down on his knees, prayed, and gave thanks to his God, just as he had done before.

—Prophet Daniel, Daniel 6:10

Two-hundred years ago, long before jets and runways, American fur traders, trappers, and explorers followed each other's footprints from Independence, Missouri, to Willamette Valley, Oregon. Most walked. Some rode horses. In time, that 2,200-mile (3,500-kilometer) path through the Wild West became known as the Oregon Trail. It was well-named because it was originally little more than a trail.

By 1840, before the railroad boom, groups of covered wagons began to overtake foot traffic. Year after year, the heavy wagon wheels dug deeper and deeper into the dirt road, creating ruts that acted like an ancient autopilot. Once your wagon wheels were in the rut, you could fall asleep and not worry about making a wrong turn. There is no way to prove it, but legend says that at a certain point on the trail, a sign was posted warning, "Avoid this rut or you will be in it for the next 25 miles."

As we consider the power of habits, I want to paraphrase that legendary warning: "Avoid certain habits, or you will be in them for the next 25 years." If we want to look at the positive side, our sign would say: "Develop certain habits, and they will be in you for the next 25 years."

The ruts on the Oregon Trail are like habits in four ways.

First, ruts and habits can be good or bad, healthy or destructive. A rut is good if the wagon is on the right trail, but bad if it is on the wrong trail. Same with habits.

Second, ruts and habits are formed by repetition. The Oregon Trail ruts were created because people repeatedly walked the same path, then rode horses on the same path. Then came the wagons—not one wagon or two wagons, but thousands of wagons over decades. Just like the Oregon Trail ruts, repetition forms deep habits.

Third, ruts and habits are formed over time, not overnight. There are no instant ruts, and there are no instant habits. Both take time to form, and both take time to fix.

Fourth, ruts and habits, once formed, are difficult to break. Remember that warning sign? "Avoid this rut or you will be in it for the next 25 miles." There are definitely ruts and habits we would be wise to avoid. There are also ruts and habits we must intentionally pursue. If we avoid destructive habits and pursue healthy habits, those good habits will possibly be with us for life.

The rest of this chapter will present three spiritual habits that are essential for church and ministry leaders, especially at the senior levels. As we look for potential successors and leaders to promote, we arc looking for these three spiritual habits. As we prepare leaders for greater authority and responsibility, we must help them go deeper with these three spiritual habits. If any of these habits are missing, we might want to delay the leadership transition or find another successor.

THREE HABITS THAT SUSTAIN MINISTRY

One of the most impactful Asbury Seminary courses for me was called "Habits that Sustain Ministry." As a person who is allergic to discipline, I was relieved to see the typical seminary offering of spiritual disciplines reimagined, rebranded, and repackaged as spiritual "habits." Discipline requires effort. Habits just happen, effort or not. For example, I always put on my left shoe first, then my right. I don't know why, but that's how I do it, every day. I don't concentrate. I don't try. I don't need accountability. I just do it that way, out of habit. Of course, habits only happen after doing something consistently for a long time, and doing something consistently for a long time usually requires discipline. But still, habits are much more palatable than disciplines, even when they encompass the exact same spiritual practices.

Perhaps Robert Mulholland had people like me in mind when he acknowledged that discipline is not a popular idea in modern Western society. He described Richard Foster's classic book,

Celebration of Discipline, as "a radical call to a largely undisciplined and comfort-seeking culture." Guilty. Mulholland continues, writing that the "avoidance of discipline" (guilty again) is currently core in our culture. This avoidance of discipline is not only in the general culture, but is increasingly in the church culture. Fearing accusations of legalism, too many pastors hesitate to challenge congregants to practice spiritual disciplines. This results in Christians who are spiritually weak and biblically ignorant.

While he is certainly not anti-discipline, Mulholland warns that for some, "disciplines become such a fixed order of being and doing that the possibility of changes in the pattern becomes unthinkable." This becomes problematic for spiritual progress when "disciplines become the total content of their relationship with God and works righteousness the shape of their spirituality." It is so easy and so common for good practices, good disciplines, and good habits to somehow become completely divorced from the gospel, and thus become a poor substitute for a dynamic relationship with God. Perhaps this discipline/gospel disconnect explains why many Christians dislike spiritual disciplines.

Mulholland is not alone in his call for a return to spiritual disciplines. I have been challenged by other authors as well, with a call to live a more attentive life, a more present life. Who hasn't felt frustrated because of their "wandering mind" while attempting to practice an attentive life? We all need to develop habits that enhance and protect our ability to be present as we seek the Lord. One of my morning go-to moves to combat a wandering mind includes noise-canceling headphones and my Spotify playlist of classical music, movie scores, and Tagalog pop and hip-hop songs.*

Henri Nouwen wrote about the same ideas using the phrase "spiritual formation." I first encountered Nouwen three decades ago at Asian Theological Seminary. At the time, I was struggling with my lack of love for spiritual disciplines. By presenting not

---

* My Tagalog playlist includes Kitchie, Moira, Barbie, and Quest.

only a new language, but also a new perspective and a clear outcome, Nouwen helped me reengage ancient spiritual disciplines with newfound energy. I re-encountered Nouwen a few years ago because of Asbury's "Habits that Sustain Ministry" course. Nouwen's classic *Spiritual Formation: Following the Movements of the Spirit* is not about steps to enlightenment. Rather, it is a book about practices that form the heart.[2]

Others have also helped frame my view of spiritual habits as a journey towards something—something foundational for spiritual leaders. As followers of Jesus, we desire to know him more fully and to experience ongoing heart formation.

When we are considering leaders who aspire to greater leadership responsibility, we must look for leaders who have sanctified hearts and skilled hands, but who also pursue the disciplines, attentiveness, and habits that form sanctified hearts.

In my opinion and in my terminology, here are the top three formative habits that every spiritual leader must develop: 1) public worship, 2) personal devotion, and 3) private service. If we want leaders to carry more leadership weight, then we must help them develop these three spiritual habits until they become inescapable deep ruts. If these habits are in decline or nonexistent, then we are considering the wrong person or the wrong timing for a leadership promotion. Let's look at each of these habits more closely.

1. The Habit of Public Worship

Since the leadership runway is a succession strategy for churches and ministries, the spiritual formation of emerging leaders is a central focus. As mentioned in our last section, spiritual leaders are developed through a combination of worship, devotion, and service. Two of these big three are communal, not individual. Only personal devotion is best done alone. Worship and service are best done in community.

When I write or talk about public worship, I am talking about much more than the singing part of a Sunday church service. Public worship begins with a formal or an informal call to worship, or a call from the secular world to a sacred place. When gathered, we worship God together in song, sermon, sacraments, and supplication. Then we are sent back to the world as witnesses. I am convinced by Scripture that a leader cannot protect a sanctified heart apart from the habit of public worship.

It seems absurd to ask the following questions, but in today's ministry world where church participation is often optional (even for pastors who hang out in a green room until time to preach) it is better to ask now than to be surprised later. Have the emerging leaders in your church or mission organization developed the habit of public worship? Do they regularly attend? Do they actively participate? Do they set an example of public worship that you want others to follow?

Tragically, it is becoming increasingly common for church and ministry leaders to neglect public worship. A few years ago, I was the guest preacher at a megachurch. I had read the pastor's books and got to meet him in person the previous year at a conference where we were both guest speakers. About fifteen minutes before the first service, we were chatting in the backstage green room surrounded by a cornucopia of fresh fruit, nuts, granola, and a variety of specialty coffee and exotic tea products. Call me ignorant, but until that moment, I was not aware that churches even had green rooms. As soon as I heard the music start, I instinctively stood and quickly made my way toward the massive auditorium. The pastor stopped me and said, "No hurry, we still have fifteen or twenty minutes." I didn't understand. It sounded like the worship service was already starting. Then I realized that this pastor had no intention of joining the singing part of worship. He motioned for me to sit down and said he had a couple more questions about discipleship.

I answered his questions as quickly as possible, hoping to get to the worship service that was already in progress.

Eventually the pastor determined it was time for our entrance, and the whole congregation watched us walk to the front row during the final song. The pastor greeted the congregation, received the offering, made some announcements, and introduced me. I preached. Using a backstage door to avoid congregants, we went straight to his green room where more fancy coffee, fresh fruit, and designer granola was waiting for us. Fifteen minutes later, when I heard the first worship song, again I stood and walked toward the auditorium. The pastor said, "Wait, we have plenty of time, and I have more questions." Continuing toward the door, I responded, "We can talk discipleship over lunch. I preach better when I worship God with the congregation." He reluctantly followed me and fully participated in the worship service. I believe it was good for his soul (to worship God in song), and for his people (to see their pastor worship). Over the next few years, I experienced a similar situation three times in three different megachurches in three different nations. This is not the example we want at the highest levels of leadership.

Contrary to this low view of worship are the words that legendary theologian J. I. Packer tweeted six weeks before his death: "Worship requires weighty words." Perhaps when Packer wrote this, he was referring to the Old Testament word for "glory" which can mean "weighty" or "heavy." True worship is glorious and heavy and weighty, and thus requires words that are glorious, heavy, and weighty. The habit of public worship pulls us out of the world of profane words to a place of heavy, weighty, glorious, and sacred words.

While personal devotional worship is a vital part of spiritual life, the weekly worship service is by design neither private nor personal, but public and communal. Public worship is a "we" experience. The Nicene Creed begins with the phrase, "We believe

..." Along with the call to community, many modern worshipers are drawn to historic Christian liturgy because of clarity and certainty found in ancient creeds and prayers. Don't underestimate the power of biblical certainty and theological clarity in our age of deconstruction and doubt. Being in community and participating in worship traditions that are 2,000 years old brings a security, stability, and surety that is woefully missing in today's volatile and unstable world. Our churches and mission organizations deserve leaders who understand this.

2. The Habit of Personal Devotion

Healthy personal devotional habits are hard to break, even in life-and-death situations. Daniel had risen from the bottom to the top of Babylon's leadership structure without compromising his core Jewish religious convictions. After foolishly listening to his ungodly advisors, King Darius signed a document demanding periodic idolatry. Anyone who did not comply would be "cast into the den of lions." Ignoring the new law and not fearing the hungry lions, Daniel continued his habit of daily devotional prayer. "Three times a day he got down on his knees, prayed, and gave thanks to his God, just as he had done before" (Daniel 6:10). Like I said, good habits are hard to break.

Throughout history, the practices of personal devotion have included prayer, worship, and Bible reading. For Daniel, his devotional habit seemed to be centered on prayer three times each day. For others, daily devotions are built around Bible reading or worship. The habit of personal devotion is more important than the method.

Eugene Peterson likens reading the Bible to a dog working a bone. The dog gnaws the bone, then buries it. The next day the dog digs up the bone, gnaws it, and buries it again. This process repeats itself for weeks.[3] When a leader consistently approaches Scripture like a dog with a bone, healthy spiritual formation and heart transformation happens. According to twelfth century monastic leader Bernard of Clairvaux, "Spiritual reading and prayer are the arms by which hell is conquered and paradise won."

My experience tells me that Saint Bernard was on to something. Augustine, Origen, Jerome, Thomas Merton, and many other luminaries in church history practiced and wrote about "spiritual reading" or *Lectio Divina*.

For 15 centuries the Rule of Saint Benedict has prescribed *Lectio Divina* as rule (a ruler to measure not a law to obey) by which spiritual progress can be motivated, monitored, and measured. The central idea of *Lectio Divina* is to read Scripture not as a text to be analyzed academically, but as the living word of God or the voice of God to be heard and heeded. Traditionally there were four steps: read, meditate, contemplate, pray. Somewhere in the past 15 centuries, a fifth step was added: action. We moderns like to skip straight to the action.

Ultimately, Scripture is what prepares the heart to lead. Good hearts tend to wander, harden, and break. Therefore, the habit of consistent Bible reading is vital to refocus the wandering, soften the hard, and heal the broken heart. If a devotional habit with a Latin name is too mystical for some, then perhaps a pattern that sounds more modern will help, like S.O.A.P.: Scripture, Observation, Application, Prayer. Or my preferred daily Bible reading method, R.O.A.D: Read, Observe, Ask questions, Do.

Here's the point: no matter what you call it, all leaders need to establish daily personal devotional habits. Do the emerging leaders we are considering for greater spiritual leadership position have a habit of personal devotion? Do they seek first the kingdom of God and his righteousness? Do they know how to hear from God? Do they have a habit of daily Bible reading and prayer?

3. The Habit of Private Service

Many years ago, while visiting the home of a missionary friend who leads a megachurch in an Asian nation, I noticed that he seemed to know the names of many of the street kids in the area. These young boys and girls were obviously poor, but they were all happy to see my friend. Later, I asked him how he knew all their names. He tried to change the subject. That made me even more curious. Eventually, he admitted that he and his wife feed, clothe, and help fund the education of many of these underprivileged kids. He refused to divulge just how many. In response to one of my questions, he made it clear that this was not a church outreach, rather this was something that my friend and his wife did, "unto the Lord." He then asked me not to tell anyone about what he and his wife were doing for these kids.

I was confused. He explained that he did not want this to turn into a church program, and he did not even want his church to know about it. When I asked, "Why?" he explained, "We are professional Christians. Everything we do is because we are called to ministry. But caring for these kids is the one thing in my life that has nothing to do with my call to ministry. This is all about my love for Jesus. This is my way of serving Jesus by 'doing it unto the least of these.' Please don't tell anyone."*

In his most famous and controversial sermon, Jesus warned religious people about the danger of making public what should be private. "Beware of practicing your righteousness before other people in order to be seen by them" (Matthew 6:1). Everyone who claims to know God is expected to practice righteousness—to pray, give generously, and serve others. The issue is doing religious things in public that should be done in secret. The other problem is the motive, which can be about serving others or impressing others.

---

*I never told anyone. I only wrote it in this book. But you'll never guess who. Pursue his example, not his name.

The sermon continues, "But when you give to the needy, do not let your left hand know what your right hand is doing, so that your giving may be in secret. And your father who sees in secret will reward you" (Matthew 6:3-4). My friend understood the power of private service and the danger of public service. He was serving all those kids in secret to please God, not to impress people. My friend was practicing the "for the sake of others" part of spiritual formation according to the Mulholland definition: "Spiritual formation is a process of being conformed to the image of Christ for the sake of others."[4]

The higher the leadership level and the more the leadership responsibility, the more important it is to have something, some type of service or generosity that is private, only known by God. This is one of the secrets to maintaining a healthy heart before the Lord. Do our emerging leaders and potential successors have a habit of private service, or do they serve only to improve their social media image?

THE LEADERSHIP RUNWAY 

As we consider spiritual leaders who can potentially carry more leadership weight in our churches and ministries, educational credentials and ministry accomplishments are important but inadequate for promotion. The starting point for established and emerging leaders must be hearts that have been set apart for God, and consecrated for his purpose. Sanctified hearts are formed and protected by three foundational spiritual habits: public worship, personal devotion, and private service. These habits not only form the heart and prepare the leader, they also aid in developing skilled hands.

Formative leadership habits do not happen effortlessly and overnight. Like the Oregon Trail ruts, good habits require time and repetition. When fully formed, healthy habits have the power to transform hearts and upgrade skills.

CHAPTER 7

Perceiving Sacred Callings

"You would not have called to me unless I had been calling to you," said the Lion.

–C.S. Lewis, *The Silver Chair*

Consider your calling, brothers: not many of you were wise according to worldly standards, not many were powerful, not many were of noble birth. But God chose what is foolish in the world to shame the wise; God chose what is weak in the world to shame the strong.

–Apostle Paul, 1 Corinthians 1:26-27

Landing a fighter jet on a floating runway on a giant boat in the ocean is one of the many difficult and dangerous skills a navy pilot must master. The only thing more difficult and dangerous is being shot by an enemy jet, while attempting to land on a giant boat.

Since its inception in 1969, the United States Navy Strike Fighter Tactics Instructor program, SFTI for short, not only invites the best of the best navy fighter pilots, but also the most experienced and knowledgeable instructors. The training focuses on air-to-air dogfighting skills, but because landing safely on an aircraft carrier is a life and death matter, mastering landing skills is also a top priority. Recognizing that the name SFTI was the opposite of cool, pilots immediately gave it a nickname: "TOPGUN."*

The 1986 film *Top Gun*—starring a young Tom Cruise flying a Grumman F-14 Tomcat—made the SFTI TOPGUN school famous. Thirty-six years later the sequel, *Top Gun: Maverick*, featured an ageless Tom Cruise flying a Boeing F/A-18F Super Hornet and introduced the TOPGUN program to a new generation of moviegoers.

In the context of our leadership runway aviation metaphor, several lessons from the Tom Cruise *Top Gun* movies are easily applicable to ministry succession.

Training the trainers. The TOPGUN program was established to improve the air-to-air dogfight kill ratio** and to train more and better trainers. The hope was that better trainers would produce better pilots. Likewise, the leadership runway strategy not only prepares future ministry leaders, but also trains the trainers who will design better ministry succession plans.

Landing the plane. How is it possible to safely land a 50,000-pound (24,000 kg) jet traveling at 150 miles per hour (240 kph) on a floating 315 foot (96m) runway in only two seconds? The answer

---

* While Hollywood writes the SFTI program as Top Gun, the Navy spells it TOPGUN. I'm going with the Navy on this one.
** Which dropped from 12:1 during WWII to only 4:1 by 1968.

is a well-trained highly skilled pilot, plus one tailhook and four cables. The tailhook is attached to the jet. The four cables are attached to the landing deck. In order to stop the plane, the pilot must snag one of four steel cables with the tailhook, otherwise we have ourselves a runway disaster (remember the first chapter?). Failure to land before running out of gas or dying is unfortunately relatively common in the ministry world. Sometimes safely landing the leadership plane requires a tailhook and multiple cables to help the experienced leader avoid overshooting the runway. Since every ministry leader will eventually land, it seems reasonable that landing would be a basic component of leadership development. Unfortunately it is not. Hopefully this book will help experienced leaders and emerging leaders have rational discussions and rigorous debates regarding landing and take-off (aka succession and transition). Landing on the runway in a safe and timely manner is so important that I have written a whole section to address the concept: "Part IV: Preparing Experienced Leaders to Finish Well."

Inviting the best. TOPGUN training is not for any and every pilot. To participate in the program, a pilot must be selected and invited by their commanding officers. TOPGUN is a "don't call us, we'll call you" school. By inviting only highly accomplished, highly motivated pilots to be trained by only the best trainers, the TOPGUN graduation rate is over 90%. In ministry succession, when we protect sanctified hearts, promote skilled hands, pursue spiritual habits, and perceive sacred callings, we create a proverbial "graduation rate over 90%" for emerging leaders to succeed in their new roles. Like the pilots invited to the TOPGUN program, top ministry leadership positions are not for whomever, but only for leaders specifically invited (called) by God.

The rest of this chapter will focus on point three—inviting the best, or in ministry terms, perceiving sacred calling. There is a major difference between officers *inviting* pilots versus pilots *volunteering* themselves. Ministry leaders are not invited; they are called by God. In the original *Top Gun* movie, Lieutenant Pete "Maverick" Mitchel (played by Ethan Hunt) and his nemesis Lieutenant Tom "Iceman" Kazansky (played by Doc Holiday) didn't just show up at the Marine Corps Air Station Miramar as walk-ons. They had to be vetted, selected, and sent by their commanding officer, Tom "Stinger" Jardian (cranky old bald dude). Vocational ministers refer to the invitation to leadership as a sacred calling. While we appreciate the spirit of volunteerism, in the highest levels of ministry leadership, a sacred call is mandatory.

But how do we know if a calling is sacred or selfish, divine or demonic, eternal or earthly? And how do we know if that called person is ready to carry the weight of next-level leadership? How do we recognize a real calling? Again, we look to David for answers.

DAVID'S SURPRISE CALLING

To better understand and perceive the sacred call, we will re-examine the leadership calling of David. His journey from shepherd of sheep to King of Israel included victories and defeats, highs and lows, friends and foes, good times and bad times, life and (near) death experiences. David's leadership journey was a long and painful process of divinely directed leadership formation that started with and constantly focused on the heart.

To understand the heart of spiritual leadership, we now turn again to a key Bible text about David's calling that includes the symbiotic relationship between David's "upright heart" and his "skillful hand."

> **He chose David**, his servant and took him from the sheepfolds; from following the nursing ewes **he brought him** to shepherd Jacob his people, Israel his inheritance. With **upright heart** he shepherded them and guided them with his **skillful hand**. (Psalm 78:70-72)

We talked about the heart and hands in the past three chapters, but this passage also connects to the sacred calling to lead people.

Called for a Specific Purpose

"He chose David, his servant" (Psalm 78:70). When God "chose David" as the future leader, those who knew him best were shocked. Apparently no one saw David's leadership potential. That didn't matter because God did. God needed a leader to replace King Saul, and he called David for that specific purpose.

David's preparation for his divine purpose was initiated by God, not by David or Jesse or Samuel or any human. Spiritual leadership always starts with a sacred call, not human vision, voting, or volunteerism. If a leader has not been chosen by God for a particular purpose, there's no point in promoting them, no matter their educational credentials or leadership charisma. Spiritual leadership preparation starts with a recognition of and a response to God's divine purpose. God initiates. Humans respond. That's how sacred calling works.

Called to a Specific Place

A divine call is usually an assignment to a specific place. Eugene Peterson refers to this aspect of calling as the "gift of place." For a few years my "gift of place" was Starkville, Mississippi. For a few decades it was Manila, Philippines. For now, it is Nashville, Tennessee. I would not have chosen any of these places, but I'm glad God did. Underlining the importance of place, Peterson insists that "theology divorced from geography (place) gets us into nothing but trouble."[1] The same trouble happens when calling is divorced from place. Just ask Lot, or Jonah, or Abraham—called men who wasted time in the wrong place. From the beginning, calling has always been connected to place. "God took the man and put him in the Garden of Eden to work and keep it" (Genesis 2:15). The place of service was God's choice, not Adam's. Likewise, God picked Abram's place of service. "Go from your country and your kindred and your father's house to the land that I will show you" (Genesis 12:1). God also picked places of service that the following individuals would have never picked: Joseph's place of service was Egypt, Daniel's place was Babylon, Jonah's place was Nineveh, and Paul's place was a Roman prison. Prison didn't change or delay Paul's calling, it simply changed the way he carried it out. The apostle to the Gentiles preferred to do ministry face-to-face, but because prison was his place of service, he wrote letters. What he preferred to do himself, he delegated to Timothy, Titus, and others.

God's call took David from the sheep pasture to the battlefield to the king's palace. David seemed perfectly content in the pasture, writing songs and defending his flock from hungry predators. Nevertheless, because his heart was sanctified, he embraced the place ordained by God.

Leaders who are considering a new role must discern if God is calling them to a new place. Place matters to God. Does the succession candidate have a heart for and a call to the new place? As this chapter is being written, the Every Nation Apostolic Council and the Every Nation Global Team are beginning conversations about potential successors for me. One question consistently comes up: Will the next Every Nation president have to move to Nashville, or will the global office move to wherever that person lives? Or can the next president lead the global office remotely or by commuting? These questions matter, because place matters.

Called to a Specific People

"He brought him to shepherd Jacob his people" (Psalm 78:71). Calling is connected to purpose, place, and *people*. David's first job was shepherding sheep, then God called him to shepherd people. No matter the type of organization, ultimately, leaders are leading people. And it is good to never forget that the people we lead are "his people," not our people. The higher the leadership position, the greater power a leader has to either build up or tear down people.

In Scripture, God's people are often referred to as sheep or flocks and God's leaders as shepherds. In Psalm 23, David paints the picture of God as shepherd and God's people as his sheep. As a shepherd, God guides, leads, protects, and provides for his sheep. In John 10, Jesus identified himself as "the good shepherd," and as such, he guides, leads, protects, and provides by "laying down his life for the sheep." This sacrificial shepherding model of leadership is contrasted with the selfish hired-hand leadership that "sees the wolf coming" and immediately "abandons the sheep and runs away." Jesus explained that selfish shepherds run away because they are "unconcerned about the sheep."

In John's last chapter, Jesus used shepherding language to recommission one of his disciples who had abandoned his calling. "Feed my lambs…tend my sheep…feed my sheep" (John 21:15-17). In his letter to the church at Ephesus, Paul listed "shepherds" as one of the five gifts God gave to equip his people for the work of ministry. Finally, Peter, the fisherman who was recommissioned with shepherding language, now exhorts other leaders to "shepherd the flock of God that is among you" (1 Peter 5:1-5). In short, spiritual leadership is like shepherding—people, not sheep. God's people, not ours.

Sometimes God calls a leader to a people and place that the leader would never pick. Sometimes the fit does not make sense, at least on the surface. That's what happened when God called Jonah to the Ninevites and Paul to the Gentiles. (And me to the Filipinos.) When this happens, there is no way the leader can take credit for the success. It is obviously all God's grace. Other leaders are called to serve a people and a place that is familiar, like when God called Peter to the Jews. No matter if the people to whom God calls us makes sense or not, the leadership call is a call to lead people.

In the context of leadership transition, we must ask if this potential successor is called to lead these particular people.

THE HEART OF THE CALL

"With upright heart he shepherded them" (Psalm 78:72). According to the psalmist, David's leadership flowed from an "upright heart." Likewise, when picking David rather than his brothers, Samuel insisted that God told him, "Do not look on his appearance or on the height of his stature, because I have rejected him. For the Lord sees not as man sees: man looks on the outward appearance, but the Lord looks on the heart" (1 Samuel 16:7). The heart of the call is the human heart.

Chapter 4 covered how important it is for every emerging leader to protect their heart. This chapter guides the established leaders to understand and discern the heart of the emerging leader as a potential successor. We now turn to three aspects of the heart in order to perceive if an emerging leader is indeed called to be our successor. Every leadership candidate must have a heart for God, a heart for God's people, and a heart for God's mission.

A Heart for God

When Samuel informed King Saul that his rule was coming to an end, he explained, "The Lord has sought out a man after his own heart, and the Lord has commanded him to be prince over his people, because you have not kept what the Lord commanded you" (1 Samuel 13:14). In other words, a heart after God is a heart of obedience. Saul's disregard of God's will showed that he was not a man after God's heart. Does the potential successor have a heart after God? That is the most important question, and the most difficult to answer, especially at the highest levels of leadership.

If an upright heart is a non-negotiable starting point when evaluating potential successors, how does a leader get a heart like

David's? First, an upright heart results when God sanctifies or sets apart a person for his purpose. Second, an upright heart forms when humans respond to God's call by consecrating themselves for that purpose. Divine sanctification. Human consecration. Both are necessary. Both are heart forming. The result of a person properly responding to God's call is a sanctified heart.

A Heart for God's People

In the last three verses of Psalm 78, Asaph describes David's leadership: "With upright heart he shepherded them." For the original people reading and singing Asaph's psalm, the word "shepherded" was pregnant with meaning. For modern city-dwellers, not so much. If a shepherd in David's day were to do his shepherding tasks with full integrity and an upright heart, he would feed the sheep, lead the sheep, and protect the sheep—even at the risk of his own life. The life of the shepherd was a life of sacrifice that was all about the sheep.

Jesus said, "I am the good shepherd. The good shepherd lays down his life for the sheep" (John 10:11). On multiple occasions he called his followers to lay down their lives, not for literal sheep, but for people. An upright and sanctified heart means many things, but at its core is a willingness to serve and sacrificially lay down our lives for others.

As we evaluate the leadership potential of emerging leaders, we must consider if the succession candidate is willing to make personal sacrifices for the good of others. In other words, does this person have a heart for the people of God?

A Heart for God's Mission

If our succession candidate has a heart for God and a heart for God's people, then we might have found our leader, but only if that leader has a heart for God's mission—specifically the part of God's mission that has been assigned to our specific ministry. Is this potential successor passionate about our mission together? It is a great starting point to embrace the grand mission of God, but that is not enough. The specific mission of this ministry must be understood and passionately owned. Here's another elusive but important succession question: Is the mission in the heart of this potential successor?

DAVID'S THREE LEADERSHIP ANOINTINGS

In the Old Testament, the process of becoming a priest or king in Israel culminated in being anointed in a sacred ceremony that included pouring, dabbing, or sprinkling consecrated oil on the chosen one. This oily anointing ceremony was usually a one-and-done, but not for David. As his sacred calling to be king developed, David experienced three anointings, separated by battles, betrayals, and many years. Here's a summary of David's three anointings.

Anointed by the Prophet in Private

David was the youngest of Jesse's eight sons. In a culture that was structured around sibling birth order, that meant David was not only the youngest, he was also the least in terms of the family power hierarchy. That explains why no one even invited him to the meeting with the prophet. As he often did in Scripture (and still does today), God ignored the cultural norm by instructing his prophet to anoint the youngest and least likely to lead. Our God seems to enjoy flipping traditional power structures on their heads. Here's the story:

> Samuel took the horn of oil and **anointed him in the midst of his brothers**. And the Spirit of the Lord rushed upon David from that day forward. And Samuel rose up and went to Ramah. Now the Spirit of the Lord departed from Saul, and a harmful spirit from the Lord tormented him. (1 Samuel 16:13-14)

Notice what happened as soon as the prophet anointed the future king with oil: "The Spirit of God rushed upon David," and at the same time "the Spirit of the Lord departed from Saul." This is some powerful spiritual stuff happening in an anointing ceremony. Apparently God does not simultaneously anoint and appoint two people to the same leadership position at the same time. He anoints one to replace the other. That obviously was not going to sit well with Saul, who had always assumed his son Jonathan would be his successor, but we are getting ahead of the story.

Anointed by the Men of Judah in Public

David's second anointing happened in Hebron when, "The men of Judah came, and there **they anointed David king over the house of Judah**" (2 Samuel 2:4). Hebron was part of the tribe of Judah's territory about 30 kilometers south of Jerusalem. The territory of Israel was north of Judah and consisted of the other eleven tribes. As soon as the men of Judah anointed David, "There was a long war between the house of Saul and the house of David. And David grew stronger and stronger, while the house of Saul became weaker and weaker" (2 Samuel 3:1).

Anointed by the Elders of Israel in Public

A couple of decades after he was privately anointed by Samuel as King Saul's successor, David's calling finally gets officially and publicly recognized when "all the tribes of Israel came to David at Hebron" to voice their loyalty to his kingship. They corporately recognized that "in times past, when Saul was king over us, it was you who led." Saul owned the title, but David led the people. Whether they have the title or not, real leaders are eventually recognized by the people they serve. Just as the tribe of Judah did seven years earlier, all the tribes of Israel perceived and acknowledged God's sacred call on David. (See 2 Samuel 5:1-2.) Here's the third anointing narrative: "All the elders of Israel came to the king at Hebron, and King David made a covenant with them at Hebron before the LORD, and **they anointed David king over Israel**" (2 Samuel 5:3).

David's first anointing was a private family affair, only his family and the prophet were present. David's second anointing was public, but only among the tribe of Judah. David's third anointing was public and included all the tribes of Israel. So, David was anointed first by the prophet of God, then by the people of Judah, and finally by all the elders of Israel. In the beginning, David's leadership call was only known by friends and family. In time, the whole tribe of Judah recognized the call. Eventually, every tribe recognized and accepted David, the emerging leader. That's often how the ministry leadership call rolls out today. It begins small, gradually grows, until eventually almost everyone acknowledges the call. If after many years, you are the only one who recognizes your call, you are probably mistaken.

THE LEADERSHIP RUNWAY 

Preparing emerging leaders to lead at the next level starts with the leader's heart (Chapter 4). Once we find a sanctified heart, we look for key spiritual habits (Chapter 6) that are essential to maintaining a good heart. Until a leader has a sanctified heart and basic spiritual habits, skill development is a waste of time. But when we find a good heart and good habits, adding advanced leadership skills (Chapter 5) exponentially increases our chances of a successful leadership transition.

Once we find leaders with good hearts, hands, and habits, then we have found potential successors. We now have to ask some important questions about the sacred calling before we know for sure we have found our successor. Does this emerging leader have a heart for God, for the people of God, and for the mission of

God? Is the potential successor called to this ministry's purpose, place, and people?

Having perceived the call of God on emerging leaders and having prepared them to lead the organization, we now turn our attention to preparing the organization to be led by emerging leaders.

Prepare the Organization to Be Led by Emerging Leaders

While some ministry organizations need minor tweaks to facilitate a smooth transition, those led by the founder generation must sometimes undergo significant structural, systems, and personnel changes before the transition to next-generation leaders. Entrepreneurial founders get away with leading and making changes that non-founder leaders should never attempt. That's why outgoing experienced leaders must make the unpopular and difficult changes that will set up emerging successors for success. It is usually a big mistake to leave those decisions for your successor.

Along with the big three—culture, systems, structure—other necessary changes include finances, facilities, personnel, and programs. If financial cuts must be made in order to right-size the budget, better for the outgoing leader to make those painful cuts and leave a healthy budget for the next leader. If experienced leaders know a staff member will not work well with younger leaders, it is better to retire, reposition, or remove those people before passing the leadership baton. If pet programs have run their course and are no longer mission-critical, better that they are canceled by the experienced leader than by the next leader. It is not fair to the new leader to have to make unpopular decisions right from the start. It is far better for the outgoing leader to be the bad guy.

Of course, nothing is more important to a healthy leadership transition than Chapter 8's topic, "Cultivating Healthy Culture."

Cultivating Healthy Culture

Culture wins. It wins every time. If you have a bad culture, it will win—and ruin your company. And if you have a great culture, it will also win and enable you to do great things.

—William Vanderbloemen

The righteous flourish like the palm tree and grow like a cedar in Lebanon.

—Adam, Psalm 92:12*

---

*According to the Midrash, Psalm 92 was spoken by Adam.

One of the most deadly runway disasters in US history occurred on August 6, 1997, when Korean Air Flight 801 overshot the Guam runway and crashed into Nimitz Hill, killing 229 of the 254 passengers and crew.

While the National Transportation Safety Board determined that the crash was due to poor communication and poor pilot decisions, Malcolm Gladwell laid the blame on poor "cockpit culture." In a 2013 interview in *The Atlantic*, Gladwell doubled down on his controversial "cockpit culture theory" as presented in his book *Outliers*:

> Korean Air had more plane crashes than almost any other airline in the world for a period at the end of the 1990s. When we think of airline crashes, we think, "Oh, they must have had old planes. They must have had badly trained pilots." No. What they were struggling with was *a cultural legacy, that Korean culture is hierarchical.* You are obliged to be deferential toward your elders and superiors in a way that would be unimaginable in the U.S.
>
> But Boeing and Airbus design modern, complex airplanes to be flown **by two equals**. That works beautifully in low-power-distance cultures [like the US, where hierarchies aren't as relevant]. But in cultures that have high-power-distance, it's very difficult.[1]

Could a "cockpit culture" of top-down deferential submission to a superior really contribute to the crash of a passenger jet flown by a skilled pilot and equally skilled copilot? Gladwell's answer is an emphatic, "Yes!" Here's why. When professional copilots and flight engineers relay danger warnings to a superior officer (the pilot) in a manner so indirect and passive that it is easily dismissed, then perhaps honorific cockpit culture is part of the problem.

Six other Korean Air jets crashed in the two decades prior to the 1997 Flight 801 disaster. Within two years, unresolved safety concerns prompted Delta Air Lines and Air France to terminate their partnership with Korean Air. To their credit, Korean Air aggressively addressed the issues, hiring David Greenburg from Delta to upgrade their operations. One of Greenburg's first changes was to require Korean pilots to learn English, the international language of air traffic controllers. This enabled Korean pilots to better understand communications from control towers. Also, by using a more egalitarian language (English rather than Korean) the Korean copilots and engineers were empowered to speak more boldly and directly to their superiors.

The parallel to creating and cultivating healthy ministry culture is obvious. If dysfunctional cockpit culture can cause runway disasters and healthy cockpit culture can ensure safe landings, then imagine the destructive power of dysfunctional ministry culture and the transformative power of healthy ministry culture! In the words of organizational consultant William Vanderbloemen, "Culture trumps your business idea. Culture trumps your strategic plan. Culture even trumps the competency of your team. Culture wins—but it doesn't have to be accidental."[2]

The goal of this chapter is to help you cultivate the right culture in your ministry—culture that is intentional and healthy, not accidental and deadly.

WHAT IS HEALTHY MINISTRY CULTURE?

It has been said that "Culture eats strategy for breakfast." It has also been said that "culture eats strategy for lunch." Apparently, no one is sure exactly what culture eats for dinner, but it has probably had enough strategy by dinner time, so it might eat "like a salad or something."* Culture not only *eats* strategy, many books state

---

* Sorry, but I couldn't resist the urge to include a *Nacho Libre* quote.

that culture *beats* strategy, and as quoted above, "Culture trumps strategy." While a lot has been said about culture and strategy, no one really knows who said what first. Many writers point to leadership guru Peter Drucker as the originator of the breakfast quote. If Drucker didn't say it, then he probably thought it...while eating breakfast.

So, we know what culture eats, but we don't know exactly what culture is in a ministry context. When I talk about ministry culture, I am talking about something that is communal, personal, pervasive, elusive, explicit, and tacit. I realize that every other word in that sentence is a contradiction of the previous word, but that only confirms the elusive nature of culture. Let's try to break it down.

Healthy Culture Is Communal and Personal

Communal means that culture must exist in a group of people. If it is only in one person, it's an individual preference, not a community culture. The beliefs and actions of one person, no matter how strong, do not define or create corporate culture. On the other hand, culture is **personal** as well, meaning that it must be transferred from the group to the individual and from the mission statement on the wall to the hearts and affections of real people. Unless enough individuals believe the beliefs and do the behaviors, we will not have the corporate culture that we want. Ideas that are confined to statements and policies, but never get in the hearts and souls of people, never become the actual culture.

Healthy Culture Is Pervasive and Elusive

Pervasive means that culture permeates the whole organization from top to bottom. As long as the beliefs, behaviors, and values stay in the boardroom, the C-Suites, and the executive teams, they are not the real culture. Once those beliefs, behaviors, and values trickle down, around, and back up, then we have a culture that will eat strategy for breakfast, lunch, and maybe even for dinner.

The flipside of pervasive is **elusive**. While culture is everywhere, it is also difficult to wrap our hands around it. It is like the air we breathe or the water a fish swims in. That's why it is sometimes easier for outsiders to discern and explain an organization's culture. Leaders get so used to the air and water of culture that they usually don't even notice. Outsiders notice it because they are not used to seeing or experiencing it.

Healthy Culture Is Explicit and Tacit

Explicit refers to the need for culture to be clearly and constantly displayed, demonstrated, and stated. While culture is always lived, it is not always written or stated clearly. Clear, explicit communication helps clarify the organization's value and desired culture.

Though clear communication is vital, good and bad culture is always in plain sight and impossible to hide. That's why I say ministry culture is often **tacit** as well, proving that sometimes unwritten implied values are more powerful than those enshrined on the website. Leaders must be vigilantly aware of the tacit cultural values that are being presented throughout the organization. After all, culture, even unwritten culture, eats strategy for breakfast and maybe for lunch.

Healthy or Not, Culture Happens

According to Maynard Webb, "Culture develops whether you design it or not." Therefore, leaders must be intentional about shaping culture from day one of their leadership tenure. In his book *Dear Founder: Letters of Advice for Anyone Who Leads, Manages, or Wants to Start a Business,* Webb presents several best practices for senior leaders regarding cultivating healthy culture, two of which are particularly applicable to a ministry context. First, "Don't pick somebody else's culture and adopt it as your own." Because "authenticity matters," we can't just borrow a fad culture-of-the-month that seems to be working somewhere else.

Webb warns that "copycat cultures," even those that seem popular, "will never last." Second, Webb instructs leaders to "consider how your culture might evolve as the company changes and grows." A ministry culture that works with one location and five employees might not work with 50 locations and 500 employees. When he was COO of eBay, Webb said the task was to "figure out how to stay true to our core values while being open to changing some of our practices." He suggests that during seasons of explosive growth, leaders should "do a culture check every six months" to determine if we are doing things that worked in the past, but need to change to foster future growth.[3]

CULTIVATING AND FLOURISHING

This might be a good time to explain this chapter title. What do I mean by "Cultivating Healthy Culture"? What does healthy culture look like? Every leader who actually leads a team, knows that healthy culture happens intentionally, not organically. According to Webb, "your company will have a culture. You can take overt action to assert and live the culture you want, or it will grow organically."[4] Ministry culture is like your garden—when unattended, good plants die, and ugly weeds organically grow in their place. When healthy culture is unattended, right beliefs and good behaviors disappear, and suddenly, like weeds growing in a neglected garden, wrong beliefs and bad practices replace them. Gardens require cultivation in order for the right plants to flourish. It is the same with church and ministry culture: cultivation is required. Leaders must cultivate the culture of their organizations in view of healthy growth and abundant harvest.

Cultivating Plants that Flourish

In May of 2020, I was invited to preach (via Zoom) at our Every Nation Europe leadership conference. My assigned topic was

"Flourishing as a Leader." Great. Of all the myriad of leadership topics, I get this one. Apparently, the conference organizers were not aware that the word "flourishing" has never made its way into a conversation, sermon, book, blog, or tweet with my name attached. Or maybe they did know. Either way, I quickly dove into the Bible looking for a way to preach about "Flourishing as a Leader," whatever that might mean. It didn't take long before I hit the jackpot in Psalm 92.

To explain what I discovered about flourishing, let me start with a tale of two plants. While I was preparing my flourishing sermon, my wife and I were planting our spring flowers and summer vegetables in our backyard. Our six-year-old granddaughter was "helping," which always makes a task a bit more time-consuming and exponentially more enjoyable. Somewhere in the process, she decided we needed a new flower, and she does not readily take no for an answer. So, of course, I took her to the garden center a few kilometers from our house, where we perused at least 100 species of flowers, all rejected by her. Finally, it was love at first sight. As soon as she laid eyes on the dark-eyed fuchsia, she had to have it.

I bought it, took it home, repotted it, watered it, and took photos of my granddaughter with her beautiful fuchsia-colored flower. But all was not well. It didn't seem to be flourishing. Within a week, it looked dead. But as I diligently and desperately did everything Siri and Google told me to do, it came back to life, then it started blooming, and blooming, and blooming.

A few weeks later, my sons and daughters-in-law showed up at my house in a large truck containing a 15-foot-tall dogwood tree. It was a surprise birthday gift. They dug a big hole in my front yard and planted the dogwood. One daughter-in-law explained that I would need to water it daily for the first two weeks, otherwise it would not properly bloom next spring. Tragically, her own dogwood only blooms on half of its branches because she neglected to consistently water it when she planted it four years prior.

I did exactly as instructed, and like my granddaughter's dark-eyed fuchsia, my dogwood started to flourish before my eyes. And that brings us to Psalm 92, which mentions "flourishing" three times.

First, and surprisingly, we are told that "the wicked sprout like grass and all evildoers flourish." What? Did I read that right? All evildoers flourish. Huh? The power of common grace, I suppose. The rest of the passage explains that though the wicked sprout like grass, **their flourishing is temporary**, and their judgment is eternal. They flourish for a season, but eventually God's enemies shall perish and are doomed to destruction forever (Psalm 92:7-9). In short, the wicked flourish but perish. The flourishing of the righteous is radically different.

We want more than a flourishing culture. Our churches and ministries want a flourishing culture that continues to flourish even when the founding generation is no longer actively leading.

Flourishing Like an Old Palm Tree

When the psalmist says that "the righteous flourish like the palm tree," he is not talking about the palm trees that adorn photos of Boracay or Hawaii—a tall pole with green branches drooping from the top. He is referring to the Middle Eastern date palm which looks more like a bush. What can the Middle Eastern date palm teach us about flourishing as leaders so that the institutions we lead can also flourish? Consider this. In 2005, a palm seed, which according to radiocarbon dating was 2,000 years old, actually sprouted. Today that sprout is over 3.5 meters tall. For 2,000 years, the palm seed was dormant, seemingly dead. There was no growth, no sign of life. Then, with a little help—human-assisted germination—it sprouted. You can visit this famous palm tree in Ketura, Israel, and take a selfie with it. Of course, it is named Methuselah.

Institutional Flourishing

As surely as an individual can "flourish like the palm tree," or not, I believe churches and ministry organizations can flourish, or not. If properly and consistently cultivated, ministries can flourish, no matter how long the ministry has appeared to be lifeless. Flourishing is always possible because life is in the seed. When I think about empty ancient cathedrals in Europe and empty modern church buildings in America—places that once overflowed with spiritual life—I pray that God would once again fill sacred places and worship spaces with his presence. When I think about university campuses in Europe, North America, and parts of South America and Africa, many of which were founded to train preachers and to propagate the gospel, I pray that God would cause those campuses to flourish with the gospel again. In some cases, it has been decades or centuries, maybe even a millennium, but still God can revive churches and revitalize institutions so that churches and educational institutions flourish like the palm tree. Just like the dry bone vision in Ezekiel 37—believe it, speak it, and watch God bring new life!

Growing Like a Cedar in Lebanon

Not only do the righteous "flourish like the palm tree," the psalmist tells us that they also "grow like a cedar in Lebanon." Cedars are so associated with Lebanon that a single green cedar tree sits in the middle of their national flag. These cedars can grow as tall as a five-story building. But when Scripture says cedar in Lebanon, it is not referring to a lone tall cedar like the one pictured on the Lebanese flag. Cedar in Lebanon is a forest of cedar trees. Cedars flourish best in community, as do spiritual leaders.

The Cedars of Lebanon State Park is about 25 miles (40 kilometers) from my home in Tennessee. It covers 9,400 acres (almost 3,800 hectares). Approximately 10% of the massive state park consists of 900 acres (365 hectares) called the Cedars of Lebanon Forest, which includes cedar glades, a unique type of growth that has been able to flourish despite the thin and sometimes nonexistent soil that sits on top of limestone. When the first Euro-American pioneers settled the area, the cedar forest reminded them of cedars of Lebanon they read about in the Bible, thus the name.

Like in biblical Lebanon, the Cedars of Lebanon State Park and Cedars of Lebanon State Forest consist of a community of cedar trees, not individual trees. If the righteous are to "grow like a cedar in Lebanon" it will only happen in community.

Flourishing in the Courts of Our God

Finally, the psalmist writes that, "They are planted in the house of the Lord; they flourish in the courts of our God." While my granddaughter's dark-eyed fuchsia and my dogwood seem to be flourishing, that is not the case with the eight blueberry plants in my backyard. There are reasons my blueberries are not flourishing. First, the soil is wrong. Blueberries require acidic soil to flourish. Nashville soil is borderline acidic and alkaline. For the first few months, I faithfully put the additives in the soil hoping for a harvest of my favorite fruit, but my travel schedule interfered with my best intentions, so my blueberries did the opposite of flourishing. But even if I had been able to add all the additives to make the soil acidic, there was another problem. The woods behind my backyard is the home of deer, rabbits, and chipmunks who apparently love blueberries for breakfast at least as much as culture loves strategy for breakfast.

Think about my fruitless blueberry story as a metaphor of flourishing in the courts of the Lord. Christian people and Christian ministries flourish in the courts of the Lord just as blueberries flourish in acidic soil. Alkaline soil is the opposite of what's needed for blueberries to flourish. Living away from the courts of the Lord is the opposite of what's needed for believers and the organizations they lead to flourish. Also, just as predators—deer, rabbits, and chipmunks—devoured what little fruit my blueberries produced, spiritual predators such as savage wolves and twisted teachings are constantly doing all they can to keep spiritual leaders and ministry organizations from flourishing.

The leadership lesson is that we cultivate soil by removing stones and adding whatever the plants need to flourish. The same with *cultivating a healthy culture*. Remove the bad. Add the good. Repeat. Constantly. Cultivation also demands that we do something about the predators that live to eat the fruit of our labor. The first few verses of Psalm 92 give the context for flourishing: thanksgiving, praise, singing, and music—what we call worship today. Likewise, cultivating healthy ministry culture requires worship and the presence of the Lord. Don't assume that the presence of God is a given just because you lead a ministry. Unless we set aside staff time to pray, fast, worship, and seek God, then no matter how important the mission and no matter how valid the call, we simply will not have a flourishing and healthy culture. It must be cultivated.

THREE PRACTICES THAT CULTIVATE HEALTHY CULTURE

The leadership runway succession strategy calls for leaders who are culture-cultivators. It is possible for leaders to build a relatively healthy culture and have no idea how it happened. As we consider potential leaders for greater leadership responsibility, we must help them understand how healthy culture is created and cultivated. But first, the current leaders who will eventually land on the leadership runway must ensure that the organization the next generation will inherit already has a healthy culture. The first step in preparing the organization to be led by new leaders is to check the ministry culture for potential deadly viruses. If the culture is sick, the next leaders are starting behind the eight ball. It is the job of the experienced leader to hand off an organization that has a healthy culture.

While there are a million little things that contribute to or take away from healthy culture, these three practices are non-negotiable if we want to cultivate a healthy ministry culture.

1. Obsessive Focus

I grew up in a family of photographers. As a high school graduation gift, my dad gave me a Nikon FM—in my biased opinion, the best mass market SLR (single-lens reflex) camera ever made. The FM's manual focus and manual exposure control forced the photographer to actually understand light in order to compose good photos. If I did not take time to manually focus the lens and manually adjust the exposure, my photos would be a blurry mess. When it comes to ministry culture values, we either have focus or a blurry mess of confusion—there's no third option, and no autofocus. Healthy culture is not built by leaders who frantically bounce from idea to idea, but by leaders who know how to stay focused. Constant change of focus is the enemy of culture cultivation. Strong culture is built by obsessive focus.

2. Unapologetic Repetition

In Psalm 136 the phrase "for his steadfast love endures forever" is repeated 26 times in 26 verses, making it almost impossible to miss the point. The word "immediately" appears 59 times in the ESV Bible; 43 of those are in Mark's gospel. To make sure we feel the urgency of his gospel, Mark repeated "immediately" 11 times in his first chapter. Paul unapologetically said that "to write the same things to you is no trouble to me" (Philippians 3:1). In fact he repeated the Greek word for joy or rejoice 15 times in his relatively brief letter to the Philippians. Remember, Paul was writing from the least joyful place imaginable—a Roman prison. Paul used repetition to reinforce the possibility of joy, no matter the circumstances. Wise leaders follow the example set by the psalmist, Mark, and Paul, by unapologetically repeating important words and concepts over and over and over and over. Then they repeat them again. That's how corporate culture is cultivated.

3. Intentional Staffing

Never forget that leaders who lead churches or ministry organizations are ultimately leading people. In the book *Good to Great*, Jim Collins addressed the importance of intentional staffing with his "get the right people on the bus" principle.[5] Collins argued that great organizations start with the right people in the right seats. When we have the right people, right strategies and tactics are relatively easy to create and carry out. In other words, "first who, then what." Why? Because the right people cultivate the right culture. The wrong people destroy healthy culture.

William Vanderbloemen agrees with Collins:

> No matter how competent people are, if they don't fit our culture, they will end up hurting our company. Every person at your company influences every other person somehow, and so hiring someone who didn't fit our culture, and who wouldn't have been happy, would have had an adverse effect on every individual and every team in some way. That effect may be small, or it could be dramatic, but you have the opportunity to prevent it when you hire people. Every time you hire someone, think about how that person can strengthen the team or weaken it. You'll have more solid teams if you hire around culture.[6]

Jesus modeled the principle of intentional staffing when picking his original 12 disciples. "In these days he went out to the mountain to pray, and all night he continued in prayer to God. And when day came, he called his disciples and chose from them twelve, whom he named apostles" (Luke 6:12-13). In ministry, intentional staffing is a spiritual exercise. It starts with prayer to discern God's will.

THE LEADERSHIP RUNWAY 

The most important high-level leadership skills in a ministry context include vision casting, critical thinking, and culture building. That last skill—culture building—is the most important, not only because culture eats strategy for breakfast, lunch, merienda, supper, and dinner, but also because "culture—not vision or strategy—is the most powerful factor in any organization."[7]

No matter how compelling our history, mission, vision, or strategy, if we don't find leaders who know how to build a healthy culture through obsessive focus, unapologetic repetition, and intentional staffing, our ministries simply will not continue in strength and health. The leadership runway succession strategy is dependent on identifying and empowering leaders who have the skills to recognize, cultivate, and maintain healthy culture.

Now that we have established the importance of "Cultivating Healthy Culture" and presented three practices that maintain healthy culture, we now turn our attention to "Creating Simple Systems" (Chapter 9) and "Constructing Flexible Structures" (Chapter 10) as we continue to prepare organizations to be led by emerging leaders.

CHAPTER 9

Creating Simple Systems

Southwest is North America's most successful and profitable airline. It is also the most simple.

—Thom Rainer & Eric Geiger, Simple Church

We behaved in the world with simplicity and godly sincerity.

—Apostle Paul, 2 Corinthians 1:12

Because I spend a lot of time on airplanes, I have had many good and bad experiences with different airlines—vowing to never fly on some and doing my best to book flights on others. One of my preferred airlines started as a low-fare, no-frills budget company.

Along with me, countless travelers rate Southwest Airlines as their go-to carrier. Not only is Southwest preferred by frequent fliers; it is also loved by investors. By its 40th year, Southwest had experienced 39 consecutive years of growth in an industry that constantly experiences financial ups and downs.

In his 2012 Slate article, Seth Stevenson asked the million-dollar question about Southwest's consistent success in a notoriously complex and volatile industry: "How does Southwest do it?" Stevenson's research led him to this answer: "By keeping operations simple. Simpler operations mean fewer things that can go awry and botch up the whole process."[1]

Could "simpler operations" really be the answer to Southwest's success? More importantly, could simpler operations also help churches and ministries—especially as they do succession planning and prepare for leadership transitions?

Despite the complexity of their industry, the Southwest playbook of "keeping operations simple" includes only four basic plays:

One aircraft: Southwest only flies one type of aircraft, the Boeing 737. That means every Southwest mechanic can repair every plane in the fleet, every pilot can fly every plane, and every warehouse only stores parts for the 737. This simplicity keeps operations efficient.

Simple seating: Southwest's seating procedure, allowing passengers to sit where they want on a first-come-first-served basis, simplifies and speeds up the check-in process.

No bag fees: Southwest does not charge for checked bags, resulting in fewer carry-on bags, which leads to faster boarding.

Direct flights: Most Southwest flight routes are direct non-stop. When a plane and crew fly from City A to City B and back multiple times each day, there is less chance of missed flights and lost luggage.

If "keeping operations simple" can result in sustained success in the complex airline industry, then perhaps similar thinking could help churches and ministries. The book *Simple Church* made the case that "the healthiest churches in America tended to have a simple process."[2] While the focus of the *Simple Church* research was specifically church-based discipleship, the discoveries can be applied to all aspects of ministry. Why? Because "in the midst of complexity, people want to find simplicity. They long for it, seek for it, pay for it, even dream of it." In the words of Rainer and Geiger, "Simple is in. Simple works. People respond to simple. The simple revolution has begun."[3]

To facilitate successful ministry succession and leadership transition, certain core ministry systems must be simplified. *The Leadership Runway* is my attempt to bring "the simple revolution" to ministry succession and leadership transition. But before suggesting how three core ministry systems can be simplified, we need to understand what systems are and what they do.

E-MYTH APPLIED TO MINISTRY

During my first decade in vocational ministry, I constantly read leadership books. One of the most helpful in terms of creating simple systems was *The E-Myth Revisited: Why Most Businesses Don't Work and What to Do About It* by Michael E. Gerber.[4] Here's my brief E-Myth summary and what I learned. The E-Myth (Entrepreneurial Myth) is the mistaken idea that most successful businesses (and ministries) must be started and led by "entrepreneurial" type people who have a charismatic personality, a deep passion for a particular product, and a high-level skill in a specific field. In reality, many failed businesses (and ministries) are started by highly skilled passionate charismatic entrepreneurial people. Unfortunately, while passion, skill, charisma, and entrepreneurial instincts are great for startups, they are not sufficient to sustain a business over the long haul. Entrepreneurs often fail because of ever-changing, outdated, dysfunctional, complex, or non-existent systems. The key word in the previous sentence is **systems**.

For post-founder sustainability, organization leadership skills, especially system-building skills, are far more important than passion, charisma, and expertise. For example, Nashville is a music city that is rapidly becoming a foodie city. New chef-driven restaurants constantly open and fail. According to the National Restaurant Association only about 20% of restaurants succeed, with 60% failing in their first year and 80% closing by year five.[5] While location is frequently a contributor, lack of experience, unrealistic expectations, and an inability to manage all of the daily tasks, including both front and back of house (think systems), play a large role.[6] Unfortunately, no matter how good the food, many of the new restaurants don't survive. Restaurants go out of business, not because the chef lacked passion and skill, but because of ineffective business systems.

Just because someone is a great chef does not mean they will build a great restaurant. Likewise, there are many skilled preachers and compassionate pastors who are not able to build strong healthy churches. Many times, their failure to thrive stems from a lack of simple ministry systems.

Reading and rereading *The E-Myth* as a young church planter helped me realize that my sense of calling, my love of Scripture, and my passion for lost souls would not automatically mean that my new church would grow or even survive. Growth would require more than good preaching and sound doctrine; it would also require simple sustainable systems. For four decades, I have applied E-Myth principles to church planting, campus ministry, and global mission, and discovered that great churches do not require extraordinary preachers and charismatic leaders. Like great businesses, great churches and ministries are built by ordinary people who develop simple transferable systems. Simple ministry systems enable and empower ordinary ministers to consistently accomplish extraordinary objectives.

A significant part of succession planning and leadership transition is to prepare the organization (systems and structures) to be led by emerging leaders. This is commonly referred to as working **on** the organization versus working **in** the organization. McDonald's has spread Big Macs and fries around the world primarily because of its simple systems. In fact, it was the simple systems created by the McDonald brothers, more than the quality of the burgers, fries, and shakes that attracted eventual owner Ray Kroc's attention. *E-Myth* author Michael Gerber described McDonald's as "a systems-dependent business, not a people-dependent business. A business that could work without him (Kroc)." In his opinion, the reason the business could work without Kroc is because, "unlike most small business owners before him—and since—Ray Kroc went to work on his business, not in it."[7]

All spiritual leaders work **in** the ministry, but many fail to work **on** the ministry. They work overtime serving the needs of people, but rarely work on ministry systems and structures. They invest generous time leading and growing their ministries and little time building a leadership pipeline. In contrast, notice how Paul described the job of church leaders: "He gave the apostles, the prophets, the evangelists, the shepherds and teachers, **to equip the saints for the work of ministry**" (Ephesians 4:11). The job of the spiritual leader was not to do all of the ministry, rather it was to **equip** (ESV) or **prepare** (NIV) the people to do ministry. Doing all the ministry is the wrong work. Equipping the people to do ministry is the right work. Doing all the ministry is working **in** the ministry. Preparing people, systems, and structures is working **on** the ministry.

PARETO PRINCIPLE APPLIED TO MINISTRY

You're probably familiar with the Pareto Principle, named after the 19th-century Italian economist, Vilfredo Pareto, who discovered that approximately 80% of Italian land and wealth was owned by 20% of the Italian people. Pareto's 80/20 rule is routinely applied across disciplines, industries, and nations. Gerber applies the Pareto Principle to business systems: "Everyone in business has heard the old saying: 80% of our sales are produced by 20% of our people. Unfortunately, few seem to know what the 20% are doing that the 80% aren't. Well, let me tell you. The 20% are using a system, and the 80% aren't."[8]

That last sentence is so important that I need to repeat and rephrase it. The Pareto Principle works because "the 20% are using a system." In other words, if you want to be in the productive 20%, then you will need more than elbow grease, you will need systems. Could it be that ministry success and sustainability over a long period of time is not only dependent on hard work, passion, and expertise, but also on "using a system?"

Gerber's description of systems is helpful for vocational ministers who are attempting to create simple systems.

> A system is a set of things, actions, ideas, and information that interact with each other, and in so doing, alter other systems. In short, everything is a system. The universe, the world, San Francisco Bay, the office I'm sitting in, the word processor I'm using, the cup of coffee I'm drinking, the relationship you and I are having—they're all systems.[9]

If "everything is a system," some systems must be more important than others. In four decades of church and mission work, I have discovered three core ministry systems that are more important than the others. If we want sustained ministry success and a smooth leadership transition from one generation to the next, we must get these three systems right. If we do, they will impact all other systems in a positive way.

THREE SIMPLE MINISTRY SYSTEMS

When *Simple Church* was published in 2006, it was perfect timing for me. Our church was beginning its third decade, and we were experiencing major growing pains. After 22 consecutive years of growth, I knew our systems were no longer sufficient, but I was not sure what to do. *Simple Church* gave me the language I needed to identify and simplify key aspects of a ministry that was growing larger and more complex. More than a decade later, I went back to school at Asbury Theological Seminary, along with three Filipino colleagues. While researching "post-founder sustainability" I reengaged the *Simple Church* principles and applied them to succession planning and leadership transition.

Every growing organization has multiple systems, all constantly evolving from simple to complex. The first sentence in *The Founder's Mentality* reads, "Growth creates complexity, and complexity is the silent killer of growth."[10] Authors Zook and Allen argue that if a growing organization does not fight complexity and embrace simplicity, it soon finds itself in what they call "the complexity doom loop," which is basically an unstoppable downward spiral leading to the death of the organization. Fortunately, they offer an antidote to the deadly complexity doom loop: "To survive, companies need to make complexity reduction a way of life."[11] Like multinational corporations, growing churches and global ministries are just as prone to creating growth-crushing complexity, and the solution is the same as in the corporate world: to embrace simplicity and "make complexity reduction a way of life."

One of the more difficult tasks of leadership is to discern which core systems influence all the other systems. Once identified, these systems must be simplified, routinized, and codified for a successful leadership transition. In a church and ministry context, at least three core systems must be simplified: discipleship, leadership, and worship. If we are able to create, contextualize, and maintain simple systems for discipleship, leadership, and worship, all other church and ministry systems will benefit. Over the decades, I have worked diligently with leaders from all over the world to simplify three core ministry systems that tend to be complex. That work resulted in the following three templates, which can be adopted as-is or adapted to fit any context.

1. A Simple System for Relational Discipleship (4Es)

From the first day we landed in Manila in 1984, making disciples has been top priority. When the church was new and small, we did one-to-one discipleship. As the church grew larger, we shifted to small group discipleship. Years of doing, experimenting, defining, redefining, clarifying, and refocusing culminated in what came to be known as the 4E Relational Discipleship strategy or system. The discipleship journey of Victory Church in Manila was published in a 2010 book titled *Accidental Missionary: The Unexpected Adventures of Making Disciples*. One year later, an American publisher picked it up, did some minor editing, changed the title, and distributed it as *WikiChurch: Making Discipleship Engaging, Empowering, and Viral*.[12]

Here's the four-part simple system for relational discipleship presented in *WikiChurch*.

Engage your community with the gospel. Biblical discipleship is not primarily a program for church people, but a call to "go" to those who are not following Jesus. Therefore, discipleship starts with engaging the people in our community with the gospel.

Establish biblical foundations. As soon as people respond to the gospel in faith, we immediately begin establishing biblical foundations to prepare the new believers for the coming storms of life. (See Matthew 24:27.) The goal is for every believer to be established in the faith, in the Word, and in a church community.

Equip believers to do ministry. One of the primary jobs of the apostle, prophet, evangelist, shepherd, and teacher is to equip believers to do basic ministry. The more believers are equipped and empowered, the more they mature in their faith. (See Ephesians 4:11-16.) Too many church leaders have this backwards, thinking that maturity is a prerequisite for, rather than the result of, doing ministry.

Empower disciples to make disciples. The purpose of equipping believers to do ministry is not so they will know, but so they will do. We equip disciples in order to empower them to make disciples.

I have never met a pastor or mission leader who did not acknowledge the importance of discipleship. Yet I have met very few who are confident that they are doing it well. The discipleship problem is not due to the lack of commitment or passion, but the lack of a simple system. Everyone knows the mission is to make disciples, but few have a system that is biblical, simple, and transferable. Victory's 4Es provide an example of a simple system for relational discipleship that can be applied and contextualized anywhere in the world.

2. A Simple System for Leadership Multiplication (4I)

In large and small ministries, a leadership shortage happens when relational discipleship growth outpaces leadership development. The solution is not to slow down discipleship, but to speed up leadership development. When a church or ministry is small, the founder can single-handedly identify and develop leaders. As a ministry grows, leadership development systems can assist experienced leaders in the identification and development of emerging leaders. Leadership development systems in many ministries are either non-existent or notoriously complex. The story of how our Manila team streamlined and simplified our leadership development system was recorded in a book that I wrote with my son, *The Multiplication Challenge: A Strategy to Solve Your Leadership Shortage.**

Here's a very brief four-part summary of the simple system that was designed to solve Victory Manila's desperate leadership shortage.

Identification. Building a leadership pipeline starts with identifying potential leaders, not recruiting ready-made leaders from the outside. Sometimes potential leaders do not currently look, think, or act like leaders at all. We will find all the leaders we need as soon as we stop looking at the outward appearance and start looking at the heart (1 Samuel 16:7), and stop looking outside the organization and start looking at the potential right in our midst.

Instruction. To prepare leaders, we must do more than transfer information, we must instruct in a way that informs minds, reforms affections, and forms character. Instruction is not a temporary phase of leadership development, but the foundation for a lifelong pursuit of knowledge and truth.

Impartation. Paul wrote to the Romans whom he had never met, "I long to see you, that I may **impart** to you some spiritual gift to strengthen you" (Romans 1:11). Paul instructed from a distance by writing letters, but impartation seemed to require proximity. The Roman church needed embodied impartation from Paul to go along with the instruction that came from a distance. "If instruction is

---

*The new and improved 2024 edition now called, Rediscovering Leadership: Identity, Develop, and Multiply Leaders

focused on informing the mind, then impartation is focused on transforming the heart."[13]

Internship. Internships (also called on-the-job training) can be official or unofficial. I have conducted unofficial internships many times without the "interns" knowing they were interns. When Jesus called his original 12, he was formalizing their on-the-job training. Jesus modeled the three basic components of internship: observation (watch me lead), participation (lead with me), and evaluation (learn with me).

Adopting and adapting this simple leadership system will go a long way to solving your leadership shortage and finding your successor.

3. A Simple System for Weekend Worship (4S)

All churches everywhere—even free-flowing anti-liturgical Charismatic churches—have a worship liturgy. A liturgy is simply a plan or system for the worship service. Some worship liturgies are biblical and well-developed. Others are not. Succession planning is a great time to reconsider a church's worship liturgy. Perhaps it is time for a more robust, biblical, and historical liturgy. Maybe the standard liturgy has become cluttered and needs to be stream-lined. If changes need to be made, it is usually better for the established leaders (especially founders) to make those changes before passing the leadership baton. Often when emerging leaders make changes, especially to the weekend worship liturgy, they are seen as disloyal or disrespectful.

Here's a simple four-part system for a worship liturgy that starts with a *Call to Worship* and ends with the worshippers being *Sent on Mission*. In between being called and sent, we worship God together in song, sermon, sacrament, and supplication.

Worship in song. Singing is an important part of worship, but worship is more than singing. Throughout Church history, when God's people gathered to worship, they sang about God's nature and character. Songs were typically theologically robust and deeply rooted in Scripture. Modern worship songs are often about human emotions and religious experiences rather than divine attributes and actions. The Church used to sing together. Now, with volume cranked up and lights turned down, we no longer hear or see our church community as we sing, making worship feel more individual than communal. I suspect this shift is more because of the systems and practices we copy and pass on, rather than deep theological reflection about the role of singing in a worship service. Part of a good ministry succession plan will include a theological review of worship systems and the role of music.

Worship in sermon. If the whole service is worship, then preparing the sermon is an act of worship, preaching the sermon is an act of worship, listening to the sermon is an act of worship, and responding to the sermon is an act of worship. All of that and more is what it means to "worship in sermon."

Worship in sacrament. The three big branches of Christianity—Eastern Orthodox, Roman Catholic, and Protestant (including Evangelical, Pentecostal, Charismatic, and other modern iterations like Every Nation) all have different communion practices that flow out of their theological position regarding sacraments in general and communion specifically. As we develop a succession plan, it is a good idea to include time for theological reflection regarding the place of communion in the worship liturgy that we are passing to the next leaders. Too often, modern churches and church movements allow pragmatism to drive sacerdotal decisions that should be primarily shaped by theology.

Worship in supplication. While there are many types of prayer, the prayer that has historically had a prominent place in public worship is supplication, which involves asking God for specific answers to specific prayer requests. Examples of supplication include prayers for physical healing, relational restoration, financial provision, salvation, and open doors for the gospel in unreached nations.

In the context of church and ministry, there are countless necessary systems, but none more essential and none in more need of simplification than discipleship, leadership, and worship. The strength and health of our finance, communications, IT, HR, security, and other organizational systems depend on how well we do the ministry side of the ministry. In other words, if we learn to do discipleship, leadership, and worship well, the rest of our ministry systems will be exponentially more effective. Yes, ministry organizations and institutions need excellent operations systems. But first, we must work on our ministry systems. In church and ministry, everything rises and falls on relational discipleship, leadership development, and public worship.

HOW WE CREATED SIMPLE SYSTEMS

Each of the above ministry systems—relational discipleship, leadership development, and public worship—had their own unique complexities and were simplified over the years in different ways. The simplification of discipleship was gradual, leadership was practical, and worship was theological.

Gradual Evolution

The 4E relational discipleship system was a gradual evolution of research, trial, error, adjustment, application, and contextualization. The 4E idea had been evolving for almost two decades before I was willing to codify it in *WikiChurch*. While parts of the 4E relational discipleship system have continued to evolve in the years since *WikiChurch* was published, the essential core (engage, establish, equip, empower) remains the same.

Practical Think Tank

Victory's 4I leadership development system (identification, instruction, impartation, internship) had a radically different origin story than the 4Es. After 25 years of multiplying disciples, in 2009, Victory Church Manila experienced a critical leadership shortage at all levels of the organization. Disciples were multiplying exponentially. Leaders were not. We needed more leaders, and we needed them yesterday. We appointed a 30-member ad hoc "think tank" and convened an emergency meeting. The task of the think tank was to look back at our first 25 years and figure out what we did that had produced so many strong Filipino leaders. The result was four practical steps—identification, instruction, impartation, internship—that reignited our leadership culture. Rather than a gradual evolution, the 4Is were the result of a 3-day rediscovery of principles we had already been practicing for 25 years.

Theological Reflection

Victory Manila's worship liturgy (song, sermon, sacrament, supplication) has emerged from theological reflection and rigorous debate among some of the most experienced leaders of Victory across the Philippines. Luke described the circumstances leading up to the Acts 15 Jerusalem Council as "no small dissension and debate." The actual council meeting consisted of "much debate" (Acts 15:1-7). That's an apt description of the theological reflection that produced the 4S liturgy. I suspect that it will continue to be discussed, debated, and upgraded over the next few decades.

Whether through gradual evolution, practical think tank meetings, or theological reflection (with much debate), the important point is that the Victory Manila team worked hard and worked together to create simple systems. This is what it means to work **on** the ministry, not just **in** the ministry.

God and Systems

In his book, *The Other Side of Pastoral Ministry*, Daniel Brown warned that "without properly developed systems, a church will not be able to function and grow on its own."[14] The Apostle Paul often used the human body as a metaphor of the church—the Body of Christ. Thus, to better understand how a healthy church body should function, we can get clues from a healthy human body. We know from fourth grade biology that the human body has ten major systems that must work together for the body to function at full capacity.* These human systems are divinely designed and genetically governed. They exist with no help from us. That's not the way ministry systems come about or function. Church and ministry systems are not divinely designed nor are they automatically installed or miraculously operated. If the church body is to have functional systems, they must be intentionally designed, constantly adjusted, and humbly operated by fallen fallible human leaders. Spiritual leadership would be infinitely easier if our systems were designed and managed by God himself.

Michael Gerber taught that "systems run the business and people run the systems."[15] In a ministry context, spiritual leaders create simple systems that run the ministry, and leaders run the system.

If you think that creating systems and allowing them to run the ministry is too corporate and not spiritual enough for churches, consider the creation story in Genesis 1. Three ideas are repeated over and over. First there are the 10 "God said" statements. Then the seven "God saw" statements. And finally, after God said and saw, he "separated." But pay careful attention to how the separation happened and see if you can find a system.

The first time separation is mentioned, notice that God himself did the separating. "And **God separated** the light from the darkness" (Genesis 1:4). The next two times separation is mentioned,

---

*Skeletal, muscular, nervous, endocrine, cardiovascular, lymphatic, respiratory, digestive, urinary, and reproductive.

it is not God directly doing the separation. Rather, God created an expanse and the expanse accomplished the separation. And God said, "Let there be **an expanse** in the midst of the waters, and **let it separate** the waters from the waters" (verse 6). "And **God made the expanse** and separated the waters ..." (verse 7).

In summary, God did the work of separation himself, then he created a system—an expanse—to do the same work he had previously done. Did God need a system? Of course not. Do we need systems? Probably.

THE LEADERSHIP RUNWAY 

We expect the strategic organized types—architects, engineers, mathematicians—to build systems. Translated to the ministry world, we expect teachers and executive pastors to be systems people, while apostolic, prophetic, and visionary people get a pass and can forgo the restraints of order and systems. I found hope that this stereotype might not be absolute when I read the words of Makoto Fujimura, a Japanese-American artist who combines traditional Japanese *Nihonga* styles with Western abstraction. "It could be argued that God created order in the universe because of God's character, particularly God's love of creating. In creativity, one can argue, one needs systems and order. So in a sense, pragmatism is bound up in the order that is embedded in creation, and we can harness it when we value the discovery of such systems."[16] If a Japanese-American painter of abstract masterpieces can embrace systems, perhaps anyone can, and should.

It goes without saying, but I better say it anyway: relational discipleship, leadership development, and weekend worship all require the supernatural presence and power of the Holy Spirit. A system, no matter how simple or complex, that is devoid of divine presence and power will not result in transformational discipleship, godly leadership, or biblical worship. We need the form **and** the power, the system **and** the supernatural, the engineered engine **and** the jet fuel.

If we want to build churches and ministries that honor God (as described in Chapter 3) and have healthy ministries to hand over to the next generation of leaders, then we must create simple systems.

Constructing Flexible Structures

The stiffest tree is most easily cracked, while the bamboo or willow survives by bending with the wind.

–Bruce Lee

No one puts new wine into old wineskins. If he does, the wine will burst the skins—and the wine is destroyed, and so are the skins.

–Jesus, Mark 2:22

Have you ever looked out an airplane window while flying through turbulence at 30,000 feet? Many years ago, as a fledgling world traveler, I was a bit unnerved when I first noticed the jet wings bending, bouncing, and flapping like a bird as we hit rough air between Tokyo and Manila. As the turbulence got worse and our wings flapped faster and faster, I had visions of St. Peter and the pearly gates.

Four decades and almost four million air miles later, I am at peace in turbulence, having realized that passenger jet wings are intentionally designed to bend but not break. For example, the Boeing 787 wings can flex up to eight meters* without breaking. To help you understand just how much those wings are bending, a basketball rim is ten feet high. Imagine the wings bending more than the height of two-and-a-half basketball goals. That's a lot of flex at 30,000 feet.

Modern jet wings are thinner and more flexible than their predecessors, resulting in flights that are more fuel-efficient and less bumpy. While I appreciate fuel efficiency and comfort, the more important reason for constructing jet wings with a flexible structure is the added safety during intense turbulence. Likewise, high-rise buildings in earthquake zones are constructed with flexible materials and flexible engineering methods for one reason: safety. In the church and ministry world, turbulence and shaking (spiritual, relational, missional, financial) are a constant threat, especially during succession planning and leadership transition. Therefore, constructing flexible ecclesiastical structures is essential for survival.

THE POWER OF FLEXIBILITY

On July 16, 1990, at 4:26 pm, a magnitude 7.7 earthquake shook the island of Luzon in the Philippines. I'll never forget that moment.

---

* That's 26 feet for my American readers.

I was in my Manila home talking on the phone with a Filipino pastor, when suddenly my floor started vibrating and the books on my bookshelves rearranged themselves all over the floor. Across town, my pastor friend dropped his phone mid-sentence and ran to see if his toddler daughter was okay. Thankfully, she was.

I walked outside expecting to see chaos in my neighborhood. Fortunately, all the homes were still standing. But 170 kilometers (106 miles) north in Cabanatuan, it was a different story. The 6-story main building on the campus of Philippine Christian College (PCC) had collapsed, crushing 154 students and faculty to death, and injuring another 100.

The devastation in Baguio was worse. The Philippines' summer capital, 165 kilometers (103 miles) north of Cabanatuan and 1,525 meters (5,000 feet) above sea level, is a popular tourist destination and the home of multiple universities. The 1990 earthquake flattened 28 buildings, including the Hyatt Terraces Baguio Hotel, where more than 80 guests and staff members died.

A summary of the human devastation in Central Luzon included 1,621 dead, 3,513 injured, 321 missing (presumed dead), and 126,035 displaced. As with all earthquakes, most of the loss of life was caused by buildings collapsing and crushing people.

While on a church-planting mission a couple of years before the earthquake, I had visited both the Hyatt (for lunch) and the wood-framed auditorium in Baguio Central University (BCU) for a student outreach. Surprisingly to me, but not to structural engineers, the old rickety wood structure on BCU survived the shaking, while the shiny new Hyatt's massive concrete, steel, and glass structure collapsed.

Why did old wood structures survive a violent 7.7 earthquake while concrete and steel structures were turned into a lethal pile of rubble and dust? Answer: Flexible structure.

Flexible architectural structures enable buildings to survive earthquakes. Flexible wing structures enable jets to survive turbulence. Similarly, flexible organizational structures enable ministry and church institutions to survive all manner of spiritual and natural challenges.

Because they are trained to be spiritual leaders not organizational leaders, some of my ministry colleagues lack confidence discussing or designing organizations, institutions, systems, and structures. Perhaps pastors and ministry leaders would have more confidence addressing organizational structures if we could find the topic in the Bible. So, does the Bible have anything to say about systems and structures?* More to the point, did Jesus ever address flexible structures? My answer is an emphatic "Yes!"

Old Clothes and New Wine

While Jesus was in the beginning stages of his public preaching and healing ministry, people often compared him to the odd and famous preacher, John the Baptist. Like the Pharisees, John and his disciples were really into fasting. Jesus and his 12 were really into eating. Thus the question: "Why do John's disciples and the disciples of the Pharisees fast, but your disciples do not fast?" (Mark 2:18). Or, why don't you do ministry the way we have always done it? Or, why don't you do ministry according to our traditions? Jesus answered with three seemingly unrelated cryptic metaphors about wedding guests, old clothes, and new wine. Because I have no clue how to explain the wedding guest metaphor, we will jump directly to preshrunk clothes and new wine.

> No one sews a patch of unshrunk cloth on an old garment. If he does, the new piece will pull away from the old, and a worse tear will result. And no one pours new wine into old wineskins. If he does, the wine will burst the skins, and both the wine and the wineskins will be ruined. Instead, new wine is poured into new wineskins. (Mark 2:22-23)

---

* Paul was not afraid to use the S-word, referring to the Church as "the whole structure" in Ephesians 2:21.

Everything Jesus said regarding old clothes and new wine was about structural flexibility, either in the context of shrinkage or expansion.

Here's New Testament Professor Craig Keener's brief commentary on this metaphor: "Wine could be kept in either jars or wineskins; the latter would stretch. Old wineskins had already been stretched to capacity by fermenting wine within them; if they were then filled with unfermented wine, it would also expand, and the old wineskins, already stretched to the limit, would break."[1] In other words, expansion demands new flexible wineskins because new wine expands and old wineskins don't. Jesus did not want the new wine to be wasted, nor did he want the old wineskins to be destroyed.

In a ministry context, new wine is a picture of expansion and growth. Structural flexibility is necessary because healthy ministries tend to expand and grow. If we do not construct flexible structures to accommodate new growth and expansion, then the expansion (new wine) will burst the ministry structure (old wineskin), and the new growth (new wine) will be lost.

In ministries all over the world, I have seen the new wine of expansion and growth destroy inflexible church structures. I have also seen new growth choked to death by inflexible structures. So, sometimes the new growth destroys inflexible structures. More often, unyielding structures stop new growth. Both cases can and should be avoided. It is tragic when the old wineskins and inflexible structures survive, but the new wine and new growth do not. Every growing ministry needs a flexible structure. If no growth is desired or expected, then perhaps old inflexible wineskins are adequate.

Flexible structures are necessary not only during seasons of ministry expansion, but also in times of contraction. Throughout church history, there have been multiple cycles of growth and expansion followed by shrinkage and contraction, then more expansion followed by more contraction, resulting in more expansion. For example, the COVID-19 lockdowns caused global ministry contraction and shrinkage. For many churches and ministries, as soon as the lockdowns ended, those with flexible structures tended to bounce back with expansion, while those with inflexible structures experienced tearing and continued contraction, kind of like preshrunk clothes with new unshrunk patches.

Lest we accept an unbiblical attitude towards old preshrunk clothes, old inflexible wineskins, and old ministry structures, it might be good to remember that Jesus actually cared about both. Rather than mocking or cursing the shrunk cloth and the old wineskin, Jesus wanted to preserve both. He was against doing anything that might further tear the cloth or burst the wineskin. While there is certainly honor due to the old, we desperately need new wineskins for new wine and new structures for new expansion. So, whether our church or ministry is experiencing a season of expansion or contraction, flexible structures are essential. That's the lesson of the old clothes and new wine.

The Trellis and the Vine

Every summer, I plant tomatoes in my small raised-bed garden. Two of my three sons and their wives also plant tomatoes, among a myriad of other fruits and vegetables. Both of my sons use simple trellis structures for their tomatoes and other climbing plants. I don't. It is just too much trouble. Of course, when my plants droop to the ground and my grandkids step on ripe tomatoes, I vow to install a trellis next summer. But I never actually do it.

In America, it is common for people to use a trellis as a decorative item and room divider, especially if the trellis has a latticework design. Decorator-type people will spend time painting and beautifying the trellis, sometimes restoring an old trellis that was formerly used in gardening. While the decorative trellis might look nice, a trellis that is not supporting a climbing vine-like plant is not doing what it was designed to do. It is not helping in the growing and harvesting of fruit. When certain climbing plants are healthy, the trellis disappears behind the vines, leaves, and fruit. Even though it is not seen, it is still doing its work, supporting the plant and the fruit. Remove the trellis and the vine falls to the ground resulting in less fruit.

In *The Trellis and the Vine,* authors Colin Marshall and Tony Payne apply the trellis-and-vine metaphor to ministry. The trellis represents organizational and institutional structures. "All Christian churches, fellowships or ministries have some kind of trellis that gives shape and support to the work. As the ministry grows, the trellis also needs attention. Management, finances, infrastructure, governance—these all become more important and more complex as the vine grows."[2]

The vine represents ministry to people. Most fruit-bearing vines and climbing plants grow stronger and more fruitful when attached to a trellis. Likewise, ministry organizations tend to grow stronger and more fruitful with some type of flexible structure. The decorative trellis with no vine or fruit is like the organization that, rather than supporting fruit-bearing ministry, has actually replaced ministry and exists for itself.

While their book makes a strong case for the role of organizational structures in supporting fruitful ministry, Marshall and Payne readily acknowledge that "structures don't grow ministry any more than trellises grow vines." In fact, inflexible structures can inadvertently hinder growth. As Marshall and Payne boldly call for the building of ministry structures, they are quick to call for established churches and ministries to "make a conscious shift away from erecting and maintaining structures, and towards growing people who are disciple-making disciples of Christ."[3] Their simple message is that we need a functional trellis **and** a healthy vine, or a flexible ministry structure **and** a vibrant ministry to people.

John Wesley expressed a similar concern about inflexible dead structures in an August 15, 1750, journal entry. Wesley attributed the absence of "miraculous gifts" not only to little faith and low morals, but also to leaders who were "dry, formal, orthodox men."[4] In other words, dry formal orthodoxy is like old stiff wineskins that can not hold the new wine (of growth and expansion).

In *2000 Years of Charismatic Christianity,* historian Eddie Hyatt blames "institutionalism" for the decrease of spiritual gifts: "As institutionalism increasingly dominated the life and ministry of the church, however, their [spiritual gifts] prevalence and influence gradually diminished." While not outright rejecting all institutions and organization attempts, Hyatt clearly defined institutionalism as an "emphasis on organization at the expense of other factors." To illustrate this point, Hyatt acknowledged that the fourth century Church rightly discerned the dangers of Gnosticism and Marcionism, but it wrongly combated these heresies with "formalized worship and centralized power."[5] Unfortunately, fighting heresy by increasing institutional authority and organizational structure might have slowed the spread of heresy, but it also smothered spiritual life, leadership development, and mission expansion.

Neither Wesley nor Hyatt were suggesting that we do away with institutions and structures. Rather, they were sounding the alarm on overemphasizing structure to solve a spiritual problem. In short, the trellis is designed to support the vine, not the other way around.

FOUR FLEXIBLE MINISTRY STRUCTURES

Not all structures carry the same weight. Some are more essential than others. Some are more permanent than others. Some are more flexible than others. My research and trial-and-error experience have taught me that there are four main ministry structures that must be constructed, examined, and possibly adjusted as experienced leaders prepare the organization to be led by emerging leaders.

1. Statement of Faith

Imagine a protective fence surrounding a farm, one that keeps out predators and marks property lines that should not be crossed. A statement of faith is a structure that establishes theological boundaries to protect churches and ministries from teachers who are twisting Scripture. It guards what we preach and teach, how we strategize and theologize. Of the four essential church and ministry structures, this one should be the least flexible.

Most church websites have a "What We Believe" section that lists key doctrines and theological distinctives. Some churches adhere to and list ancient creeds and confessions. Others have a modern take on essential beliefs. A well-crafted statement of faith will accomplish five outcomes:

Orthodoxy—Affirms established doctrine, not introduces new doctrine.

Priority—Emphasizes the most important doctrines, not covers all doctrines.

History—Connects to the historic church, not separates from church history.

Clarity—States beliefs clearly, not vaguely.

Unity—Creates a platform for agreement, not dogma to debate.

It is rarely a good idea for a new leader to tinker with an established church's theological traditions or core doctrines. Therefore, if the statement of faith needs editing, clarification, or additional points, that process should be led by the experienced leaders in conjunction with the emerging leaders as part of the succession plan before the leadership transition.

2. Mission, Vision, Values (MVV) Statements

While not as inflexible as the statement of faith, the MVV statements must balance flexibility with longevity. For some ministry organizations, the mission, vision, and values are all contained in one statement. Some have one combined mission and vision statement, plus a list of values. Others have a mission statement, a vision statement, and a list of values. The MVV statements of Victory Church (the Manila church I led from 1984-2006) have undergone four changes in four decades. Some were minor tweaks, some were significant upgrades. If we constantly change our MVV statements, we will create little buy-in and much confusion. If our mission and vision can be accomplished in our lifetime, then it is probably too small and in need of an immediate and expansive upgrade. I realize that if we ask a dozen leaders to define mission, vision, and values, we will probably get a dozen different answers. Here's how I describe (not define) MVV statements in the ministry organizations I have led and those I currently lead:

Mission—Why we exist

Vision—What we do

Values—How we build and behave

No matter how you define or describe mission, vision, and values, and no matter if you have one, two, or three statements or lists, clarity and simplicity are much more important than agreeing with the experts on the technical definitions. For a healthy leadership transition, the experienced and emerging leaders must know and agree on why the organization exists, what the organization does, and how the people are expected to build and behave.

3. Organization Chart

In my experience, the org chart is the most flexible ministry structure. Growth and expansion demand flexible organizational structures, and thus flexible org charts. The faster the growth and the greater the geographic expansion, the more the org chart must flex. Organizational flexibility is especially important in smaller ministries that are beginning to grow. According to Michael Gerber, "Organizational development reflected in the Organization Chart can have a more profound impact on a small company than any other single Business Development step."[6] As high-level leadership transition approaches, the following structural tensions must be thrashed out and agreed upon as part of the succession planning discussion:

Centralization—What should be centralized, and what should be localized?

Authority—What areas of our organization need to be hierarchical, and what areas need to be flat?

Flexibility—Which systems, structures, statements, policies, and traditions are flexible, and which ones are fixed?

The concepts of centralization, authority, and flexibility are never either/or decisions, but rather sliding scales of emphasis at particular times. Like many organizational leadership experts, Michael Gerber teaches that "all organizations are hierarchical." All organizations require some type of structure. If there is no structure, we do not have an organization, but a mob. Gerber warns, "Mobs do not get things done, they destroy things."[7] No sane leader wants mob rule, so we organize and structure our churches and ministries. Often a reorg is needed before the leadership baton is passed from an experienced leader to an emerging leader. It is rarely a good idea to leave the reorg to the incoming leader.

4. Legal Boards

Management guru Peter Drucker expressed little confidence in boards when he wrote, "There is one thing all boards have in common—they do not function."[8] Unfortunately, some of my church-consulting experience confirms Drucker's cynical statement. Hopefully though, this chapter will help us do board work in a way that honors God and empowers the mission of our church and ministry institutions.

The difficulty with designing functional church and ministry boards is that the Bible is completely silent on the subject. Scripture has much to say about leaders, leadership, and leading, with no mention of faith-based non-profit boards. For centuries, churches and ministries grew and multiplied to the ends of the earth without the help or guidance of legal boards. Today in many "creative-access nations,"* it is illegal or unwise to officially register a church or Christian ministry. Since the church is not registered, there is no legal board. Unregistered churches all over the world continue to thrive without legal boards, corporation papers, and Robert's Rules of Order. I am sure life and leadership would be much simpler if modern churches and ministries could be led by apostles, prophets, evangelists, shepherds, teachers, bishops, and elders just like the ancient church. However, because in many nations we need to open bank accounts, run payrolls, sign contracts, and purchase properties, we are required to be a legal entity and to have a board of trustees. This reality means we must manage the tension of being faithful to biblical church governance while complying with national and local laws.

No matter the official rules that govern religious institutions in your nation, the following board responsibilities are a starting point. In other words, here's what your church board must do. Hopefully it will not have to do much more than this, but it must do

---

*Muslim, Buddhist, Hindu, Communist, and totalitarian nations

at least the following without encroaching on biblically qualified and spiritually gifted pastors and elders:

Financial stewardship—Focus on budgets, spending boundaries, and executive limits.

Legal compliance—Understand and meet the requirements of national and state laws that govern religious non-profit institutions.

Mission alignment—Remain committed to and aligned with the organization's mission, vision, values, and culture.

Executive oversight—Provide empowerment and oversight for the organization's top executive, based on the job description.

Succession planning—Create and manage succession planning for board members, board chair, and top executive.

The five responsibilities outlined above are not equally relevant throughout the world. Not all nations have the same legal requirements. These legal obligations are primarily carried out in nations that officially recognize Christian churches and institutions. It is important that leaders know what is required in their home country. For those who need legal boards, it is common to have the same people serve as both church elders and legal board members. I do not recommend this, as there are two completely different skill sets required for spiritual leadership and board leadership.

Spiritual leadership and eldership require spiritual maturity and clearly delineated Christian character. Board membership requires financial, legal, and organizational skills. When the same people serve as elders and/or legal board members, the line between what is required by the Bible (ecclesiastic leadership) and civil law (board governance) becomes blurry. I have found it better to go with two separate groups, with a little overlap if necessary. Remember, when the legal board meets, it has a five-fold task:

financial stewardship, legal compliance, mission alignment, executive oversight, and succession planning. Every other discussion and decision should be the domain of the pastors and elders.*

THE LEADERSHIP RUNWAY 

Having examined multiple structural metaphors (wineskins, stretchy clothes, trellises), I want to end this chapter by reiterating the biblical purpose of flexible structures: kingdom expansion.

Seven hundred years before Jesus connected expansion (new wine) with flexible structures (new wineskins), the prophet Isaiah also preached expansion in the context of flexible structures. Rather than wine and clothing metaphors, Isaiah made his point with a tent metaphor. Everyone in his audience would have been familiar with tents, tent curtains, and tent cords. Isaiah exhorted, "Enlarge the place of your tent, and let the curtains of your habitations be stretched out; do not hold back; lengthen your cords and strengthen your stakes" (Isaiah 54:2). In the time of Isaiah, a house of stone or brick could not be enlarged by stretching, but a tent was a different story. Tents could be "enlarged" and "stretched out" to accommodate more people. Why? Because unlike stone or brick, tent fabric was flexible.

Why was flexibility important? Isaiah prophesied the reason they needed flexible structures: "For you will spread abroad to the right and to the left, and your offspring will possess the nations" (Isaiah 54:3). Because of eminent expansion ("to the right and the left") and to secure a place for the future generations ("your offspring"), flexible structures (stretchy tents) were needed. If a church or ministry has no vision for expansion, global impact, or next-generation leaders, then perhaps there is no need for flexible

---

* See Appendix B: "When Legal Boards Are Required" for additional information on legal board best practices, worst practices, and board meeting templates.

structures. The old structures will do just fine. But for churches and ministries with a global and multi-generational vision, flexible structures that can be enlarged and stretched are essential.

Prepare Experienced Leaders to Finish Well

In May 2021, a small plane carrying faith-based diet guru Gwen Shamblin Lara, her husband, and five guests crashed in Percy Priest Lake near Nashville a few moments after takeoff. Everyone on board died. This crash did not have to happen. There was no mechanical failure. The plane itself was in good flying condition. The unfortunate tragedy appears to have been the result of the pilot's unforced error.

The NTSB* investigators used two technical phrases to explain the deadly crash: "spatial disorientation" and "somatogravic illusion." Spatial disorientation refers to the pilot's lost ability to discern the airspeed, altitude, or attitude of his plane. In other words, a pilot could think he is gradually flying higher when he is actually rapidly descending. Somatogravic illusion occurs when the pilot has limited or no visibility during rapid acceleration or deceleration, and rather than trusting flight instruments, he relies on personal senses (illusions). Spatial disorientation and somato-gravic illusion both have to do with trusting feelings rather than instruments during times of limited, blocked, blurred, and con-fused vision.

The application to experienced leaders during transition is obvi-ous. It is common to feel disoriented and visionless while emerging leaders are increasing and we are decreasing. Sometimes veteran leaders feel like they are about to crash, when in reality the succes-sion plan is going smoothly. If they trust their illusionary feelings, they suddenly shoot for the clouds when they should be prepar-ing to land. When ministry succession and leadership transition leads to disorientation, illusion, and confusion, it is better to rely on instruments than on feelings. *The Leadership Runway* provides

---

*National Transportation Safety Board

emerging and experienced leaders with the instruments necessary to climb, fly, and land safely with all the passengers (congregants) and planes (ministries/churches) safe and sound.

Now, in Part IV, we turn to the final area of preparation: preparing experienced leaders to avoid unforced errors.

Is My Ministry Still Needed?

Aging aircraft may prove to be more valuable than one expects.

–International Air Transport Association (IATA)

The gifts and the calling of God are irrevocable.

–Apostle Paul, Romans 11:29

Have you ever wondered what happens to retired aircraft? Thousands upon thousands find their final resting places in "aircraft boneyards," sometimes called "aircraft graveyards." If you want to pay your respects in the USA, you can visit aircraft boneyards in Arizona, California, Mississippi, and Texas. Other massive boneyards can be found in Australia, Canada, Kyrgyzstan, and Spain.

A small number of retired passenger jets will be resurrected from boneyards and recommissioned. An even smaller number will be sold to Hollywood or Bollywood to be used as TV props and on movie sets. Some boneyards attract random tourists and aviation enthusiasts who take selfies with relics from defunct airline brands like PanAm, Swissair, Aloha, or Northwest. The multi-billion dollar second-hand parts industry ensures that every retired aircraft still has worth, even those that end up as scrap metal.

I am not suggesting that retired ministers sell body parts or act as props for selfies. I am saying unequivocally that retired ministry leaders still have purpose and value, even after relinquishing organizational positions. There will always be a place for their ministry gift. Why? Because the divine call is irrevocable.

A few months before the COVID-19 lockdowns in Nashville, I had lunch with a then 86-year-old preacher who has had at least four successful ministry careers. This Oxford-trained theologian has served as a cross-cultural missionary, a long-tenured pastor, an author (with more than 50 published books!), and a conference preacher. And he's not slowing down anytime soon. More of a distant hero than a personal mentor to me, I know him primarily through his books and sermons and one unforgettable meal we shared together. While feasting on roti canai, chicken baos, and Sichuan wontons, we discussed ministry, miracles, writing, preaching, and pastoring. I learned much that will remain with me for the rest of my life.

Toward the end of our conversation, he asked a question that haunts many ministers as they consider retirement or leadership transition: "Is there still a need for my ministry?"

I answered instantly and emphatically in the affirmative, and promptly invited him to preach and teach at an upcoming Every Nation event that included leaders from all over the world via Zoom.

A few years prior to our lunch conversation, this spiritual giant had tried retirement in a popular and beautiful beach city, but his attempt at retirement didn't last long. He quickly grew tired of idyllic sunsets and bonefishing. While he had retired from his position as a pastor, and while he enjoyed paradise for a season, he quickly discovered that he could not retire from his sacred call. So he retired from retirement and got back to preaching and writing. Yet, during our lunch conversation he wondered out loud if there was still a need for his ministry.

A couple of months after our lunch meeting, I was privileged to host him on a Zoom call with Every Nation apostolic leaders from Africa, Asia, Europe, Middle East, North America, Oceania, and South America. If this retired missionary pastor had ended that Zoom meeting with his question, "Is my ministry still needed?" the response would have been an instant and unanimous "YES!" from every leader on that call.

For those wondering if there is a need for *your* ministry as you consider ministry succession and leadership transition, the instant and unanimous answer for you is YES!

In 2014, I had a similar conversation with a ministry mentor during a leadership conference where we were both preaching. We were having dinner with other global leaders who attended the conference. Everyone was commenting on my friend's sermon. Someone asked him how he had such energy at 83. His answer was, "If I ever stop preaching, I will die."

I called him while writing this chapter to wish him a happy 91st birthday. He had just landed in Hawaii to preach at a prophetic conference. (Yes, he's still a globe-trotting preacher at 91, with no intention of staying home, slowing down, or dying anytime soon.)

Like the man in the previous story, this living legend has had multiple successful careers as a teenage healing evangelist, global missionary revivalist, local pastor, prophetic minister, TV and radio preacher, and global apostolic leader. I am a better leader and human because of his input and example for the past four decades.

When talking about his longevity and energy, he always goes back to his sacred calling to preach. While he "retired" from his position as a local church pastor three decades ago, he says he will never retire from his call to preach. On many occasions, I have heard him repeat that phrase about his life and death being connected to his preaching ministry. Judging from his past few sermons, I'm predicting that he will live to at least 110!

A THEOLOGY OF RETIREMENT AND DEATH

It is common for spiritual leaders to simultaneously *believe in* retirement and *not believe in* retirement. Many believe they should retire from a specific ministry position, but not retire from the call and gift of God. The men in the two stories above both retired from cross-cultural missions and from local church pastoral positions, but not from preaching, teaching, writing, and spiritual leadership. Both of these experienced leaders intend to continue preaching and teaching as long as their bodies and minds can keep up with their vision and ministry opportunities.

Many modern pastors and ministry leaders have given little thought to retirement planning, with 27% saying they will never retire. This explains the gap between the average age of senior leader retirement in the corporate world and the ministry world. For outgoing CEOs at S&P 500 companies, the average retirement age is 58. In contrast, the average retirement age for American pastors is 65, which is 7 years older than in the corporate world. It is common for ministry founders and long-tenured pastors to hold their positions well into their late 70s and often into their 80s.[1]

There are three reasons experienced ministry leaders hold on to senior positions longer than their counterparts in the corporate world: lack of financial preparation for retirement, personal identity, and a sense of significance. Unlike most pastors, senior leaders in the corporate world typically retire with plenty of money. Also, unlike pastors who usually have their identities wrapped up in their ministry calling and receive a sense of significance from spiritual leadership, CEOs and presidents of corporations tend to move on to the next phase relatively unhindered by identity or significance issues.

For some pastors and ministry leaders, the resistance to retirement is more about theological tradition than money, identity, or significance. Some church traditions and theological perspectives allow zero room for retirement, often resulting in unintended negative consequences, including no succession plan, no clearly identified successor, and inadequate preparation of potential successors. Tragically, in the church world, the lack of a succession plan and a prepared successor sometimes leads to an avoidable split when the senior leader finally dies, and younger leaders fight for position and power.

Though the concept of retirement is not defined in the Bible, the process of leadership transition is described over and over. Some of these leadership transition narratives are instructional. Many are tragic. Some are as simple as Abraham blessing next-generation tribal leaders before he died (Genesis 19:26-29). Others are more strategic, like David making preparations for the success of his successor. David's written succession plan is described in 1 Chronicles 28-29:

- David picked Solomon as his successor (28:9-10).
- David planned the temple architectural design (28:11).

- David provided for the house of God (29:2-3).
- David prayed for Solomon's success, specifically for his heart (29:19).

These four elements in David's written succession plan are a good starting point for established organizations and experienced leaders today. Whether or not experienced leaders have a theology of retirement, they can at least follow David's example and provide a clearly identified successor (Solomon), a compelling mission (build the temple), financial health, and spiritual covering (prayer).

PAUL'S THEOLOGY OF CALLING

As experienced leaders consider landing on the leadership runway for the purpose of retirement, they must only do so while remembering and embracing their calling. Career or vocational decisions made outside the context of sacred calling are usually bad decisions.

Paul mentions the idea of the vocational ministry call four times in the first four verses of Ephesians 4:

> I therefore, a prisoner for the Lord, urge you to walk in a manner **worthy of the calling** to which **you have been called**, with all humility and gentleness, with patience, bearing with one another in love, eager to maintain the unity of the Spirit in the bond of peace. There is one body and one Spirit—just as **you were called** to the one hope that belongs to **your call**.

Here's a brief description of each time Paul mentioned calling in the text quoted above.

"Walk in a manner worthy of the calling"

Paul charged the Ephesians to live up to their calling, but he did not leave it up to them to decide what walking worthy of the calling looked like. The next verse frames walking worthy of the calling in relational terms, not in ministry fruitfulness terms. Too often, ministers wrongly look at attendance or baptism numbers to decide if they have walked worthy of the calling or not. If they have a big church with lots of buildings and baptisms, then they assume that they must be walking worthy of the call. If they have a small church, then not so much. Ministry size had nothing to do with Paul's teaching on walking worthy of the calling. For Paul, worthiness to the call was all about relational character. Notice the words Paul used to describe walking worthy of the call: humility, gentleness, patience, love, unity, and peace. All of these words are about how we treat people, not about the size and scope of our ministry.

"To which you have been called"

Paul did not say that perhaps one day in the future, if you live righteously, then maybe you will be called. No. He told the Ephesian leaders that they already "have been called" and now need to live worthy of that call. We are not called if we strive to live worthily. Rather, we strive to live worthily because we have already been called. The call of God is something that happened in our past, not something we hope for in our future. If a man or woman has already "been called," they do not suddenly lose that call when they let go of a previously held ministry position. The call is not defined by a position, title, or ministry organization. The call is defined by God and transcends official organizational employment status.

"Just as you were called"

Past tense again. Paul did not say, "so you might be called" or "in order to earn a calling." Rather, he says because "you were called." Calling has already happened, but during a leadership transition, we sometimes forget or get confused* regarding who we are called to be or what we are called to do. While Paul was not specifically

---

* Remember spatial disorientation and somatogravic illusion? See page 154.

referring to retirement, his word to the Romans certainly applies to spiritual leaders who are considering retirement from a ministry organization: "The gifts and the calling of God are irrevocable" (Romans 11:29).

"One hope that belongs to your call"

Paul's theology of calling was not only past tense, but also possessive and personal. Paul taught the Ephesians that hope was connected, not to a general calling that everyone has, but to "your" calling, a specific and possessive calling. For some ministers, the idea of retirement is an exciting adventure into a new aspect of their calling. For others, retirement from a specific position brings dark clouds of depression and an unknown insecure future. But if we start our retirement discussion with the "one hope that belongs to your call" then the dark clouds tend to vanish. Hope comes alive as we consider the future God has planned for us.

Paul's theology of calling teaches that while the divine call is not earned by the worthiness of our lifestyle, it does demand that we walk worthily through the development and display of relational character. In other words, because of our calling, we are supposed to treat people with humility, gentleness, patience, and love. Our calling and the expectations of walking worthily have nothing to do with ministry organizational employment status.

DIFFERENTIATING CALLING AND IDENTITY

It is common for experienced spiritual leaders to have their personal identity inexorably tied to their leadership position and organizational title. This happens to leaders in all vocations, but it is especially prevalent in church and ministry leadership. The longer spiritual leaders practice their ministry, the more their personal identity meshes with their ministry calling and position.

In Paul's opening sentence to the Romans, he differentiates his identity as "a servant of Christ Jesus" from his calling "to be an apostle" (Romans 1:1). His identity and his calling are connected, but distinct. Our calling to a people or place can and often does change, but our identity as God's child is permanent and eternal. Leadership transition is a time for experienced leaders to hold on to our identities as children of God while letting go of our positions and titles. When spiritual leaders fail to differentiate between identity and calling, we end up holding on to our identities and to our positions with equal grip.

Ministry leadership consultant William Vanderbloemen gets straight to the point on tangled identity: "To put it bluntly, too often pastors stay at a church not because they're thriving there, but because their identity is tied too much to their present role and they don't have anything else to put their passion into."[2] There are many reasons experienced ministry leaders find their identities wrapped up in their titles. At the top of the list is a sense of calling that led them to the position in the first place. It is difficult for spiritual leaders to separate what God calls us to do (ministry position) with who he calls us to be (personal identity). This is one reason many ministers have a difficult time talking about retirement, passing the baton, or landing on the leadership runway. The calling to a ministry is so strong that some ministers feel like they are being unfaithful to God if they even consider retirement from a position. Others have been so "all-in" that they are not sure who they are or what they would do if they acquiesce to a leadership transition.

The following four questions have proven to be helpful as experienced spiritual leaders attempt to differentiate their call to ministry from their identity in Christ. I have revisited these questions multiple times as I grow older and consider the inevitability of my own ministry succession and leadership transition.

1. Who am I called to be? (Identity)

First and foremost, we are called to be sons and daughters of God. "To all who did receive him, who believed in his name, he gave the right to become children of God" (John 1:12). Being adopted into God's family has nothing to do with whether or not we have an official position in a ministry organization. We get our identity from the Word of God, not from a religious organization. We are called to be "a chosen race, a royal priesthood, a holy nation, a people for his own possession" (1 Peter 2:9). None of these callings are diminished if and when we retire from a church or ministry organization. They predated our ministry employment and they will outlive our ministry employment. We can and should continue to be who God called us to be, no matter our organizational position or title.

2. What am I called to do? (Vocation)

This is different for all of us. My big-picture vocational calling is to do church planting, campus ministry, and global mission. My specific calling based on spiritual gifting is to teach and preach God's Word, strengthen and serve churches, and identify and develop future leaders. This threefold general calling and threefold specific calling predated my current ministry position and organizational job description, and it will outlive my current position and employment. I hope to continue preaching God's Word, strengthening churches, and developing leaders long after I vacate my Every Nation office. As succession plans are being formulated and leadership transitions are being carried out, it is more important than ever that experienced leaders find their security in sacred callings rather than organization charts. What has God called you to do?

3. Where am I called to serve? (Location)

Again, this is different for all of us. When I started in vocational ministry, I knew I was called to Mississippi State University in Starkville, Mississippi. In 1984, God called me to Manila, Philippines. While

Manila will always feel like home, Deborah and I now live primarily in Nashville. As we gradually turned over the leadership of Victory Church to emerging Filipino leaders, I felt it was important to spend less time in Manila to give the new leaders space to lead. Locational calling often changes as experienced leaders hand over leadership authority to emerging leaders. Where has God called you to serve?

4. How am I called to serve? (Character)

While we may differ in *what* we are called to do and *where* we are called to serve, the *how* is the same for everyone. If we are called, then we are all called to serve in the same way that Paul instructed the Ephesians to serve. Notice the words I put in bold. "Walk in a manner worthy of the calling to which you have been called, with **all humility** and **gentleness**, with **patience**, bearing with one another in **love**, eager to maintain the **unity** of the Spirit in the bond of **peace**" (Ephesians 4:1-3). No matter the specifics of our calling, we are called to humility, gentleness, patience, love, unity, and peace. These six words are the foundation of what I like to call "relational character." This part of our calling still applies especially during and after our leadership transition.

In his book *The Call*, Os Guinness writes, "We may retire from our jobs but never from our calling."[3] One day, we will not be in our current positions, but we will still have a divine calling. We will no longer have a title, but we will still have a calling. Although retirement might change our vocation and location, our identity as children of God and our stewardship of "relational character" will never change. The identity and gifting aspects of the call are irrevocable.

Like many before me, I have found that the requirements to finish strong in the final phase of my calling is exactly like the beginning. "Jesus told his disciples, 'If anyone would come after me, let him deny himself and take up his cross and follow me'"

(Matthew 16:24). Whether we are emerging leaders trying to start right or experienced leaders trying to finish well, we are called to a life of self-denial not self-service, cross-carrying not comfort-seeking, and following Jesus not pleasing the culture.

No matter your age, your ministry is still needed, therefore you are still called to deny self, carry the cross, and follow Jesus no matter where he leads.

THE LEADERSHIP RUNWAY 

This chapter started with a story about one of my spiritual heroes who asked a common question, "Is my ministry still needed?" If you are an experienced leader reading this book and you are wondering about that question as you consider ministry succession, let me give you a clear and emphatic answer: YES! Your ministry is still needed! Maybe not in the same position with the same title in the same place to the same people, but YES, you and your ministry are still needed. Why? Because "the gifts and the calling of God are irrevocable" (Romans 11:29).

The next chapter ("I Must Decrease") will help you understand why you might be feeling unneeded as you gradually or rapidly transition your leadership responsibilities to the next generation.

CHAPTER 12

I Must Decrease

Fame will eat the soul and your heart will break.

–Van Morrison, Rock & Roll Hall of Fame member

This is the assigned moment for him to move into the center, while I slip off to the sidelines.

–John the Baptist, John 3:30 (Message)

The first sentence in this book introduced a painful truth about real and metaphorical runways. "The deadliest accident in aviation history happened on a runway, not in the air." Likewise, some of the deadliest ministry accidents happen while attempting to land or take off on a succession runway—or worse, attempting to land or take off where no succession runway has been built.

Landing demands a decrease in speed. Taking off requires an increase in speed. If a pilot decreases speed in order to land, then suddenly decides not to land and increases speed, a runway disaster often results. In a ministry succession context, when experienced leaders announce a decrease, then decide not to land and begin to increase, the inevitable result is confusion, chaos, or crash.

While I was writing this chapter, an influential American church experienced one of the worst ministry leadership baton pass attempts I have ever witnessed. To make a tragic situation worse, it happened during a Facebook Live broadcast of a Sunday worship service. My heart grieved for the founding pastors, the well meaning but hapless elders, the emerging leaders, the church members, and especially for the new believers who are always most at risk when experienced church leaders fail to lead wisely and refuse to land well.

Here's the true story, with fictitious church and pastor names, but very real events.

No-Runway Church (NRC) started as a simple Bible study in Pastor and Mrs. A's home almost three decades ago. NRC grew gradually, then rapidly, to become one of the most influential megachurches not only in the city, but in the region. Attendees included prominent politicians, wealthy business leaders, professional athletes, and famous entertainers.

I'm not sure of the exact timeline, but more than a year before the runway disaster was captured on Facebook Live, Pastor A had announced a succession plan naming Pastor B as his successor.

The plan was for Pastor A to gradually decrease his leadership and preaching as Pastor B gradually increased his leadership and pulpit presence.

The succession plan seemed to work, until Pastor B suddenly resigned, then at the insistence of the elder board, unresigned. The details are a bit fuzzy, but the Facebook Live video was unfortunately loud and clear.

At the Sunday morning 9:30 worship service, the incoming senior pastor, Pastor B, read his statement: "Due to a lack of clarity throughout this transition, and because of the pride in my own heart, I became impatient and demanding toward Pastor A. I understand that my attitude caused offense, and for that, I am deeply sorry. I apologize to Pastor A, Mrs. A, the elder board, and the NRC congregants. The lack of clarity and the offenses from both sides have resulted in strained relationships, mistrust, and bitterness. Both sides have been wounded, reflecting poorly on our leadership, our church, and most importantly, our witness."

After Pastor B read his statement, the elders came on stage to call for a moment of prayer and repentance. That's when the runway confusion manifested. Mrs. A, the wife of the founding pastor, went off script. She walked on stage, grabbed a mic, and rebuked the incoming pastor for not being truthful, attempting to cancel the founding pastor, and for sinning against her husband. She then began asking rhetorical questions about whether or not she still has authority in the church as a cofounder. Just seconds before someone on the tech team cut the live feed, she declared, "That is the truth. You need to know th—", followed by a silent blank screen.

Wisely, the 11:00 a.m. service was canceled, and the video of the service has since been removed from the church's Facebook page.

Within 24 hours, the elder board posted a public statement on the church website to denounce the outburst from Mrs. A, adding that they were disappointed and embarrassed by her conduct.

Pastor A released his own statement on his Facebook page explaining he and Mrs. A were moving on from the church and would no longer preach, teach, or attend No-Runway Church that they had founded almost three decades ago. "My wife is a courageous woman of God. She shared only the tip of the iceberg regarding Pastor B and the current leadership team's disgraceful actions towards our family. I support everything that she shared."

I don't know who was right and who was wrong. In messy church situations, there is usually plenty of blame to go around. What I do know is that when leaders get offended and lose trust during a leadership transition, a runway crash usually follows. Sometimes, the problem is an emerging leader's failure to launch. In the case of No-Runway Church, the problem looks like an experienced leader's failure to land. It is not uncommon for experienced pastors to sense the need to land the plane, then for some reason, they decide to increase speed when they should be decreasing. A failure to land causes confusion, mistrust, and resentment in the emerging leader.

I MUST DECREASE: A PRAYER AND A PROMISE

There will never be a perfect succession plan or perfect leadership transition, not as long as fallen, fallible humans are involved. The closest to a perfect leadership transition we will ever find are the two leadership transitions that involved Jesus (and fallen, fallible humans). In his first transition—one that we talked about in Chapter 1—Jesus was the emerging leader and John the Baptist was the established leader. In his second transition, Jesus was the established leader. The disciples were the emerging leaders.

Since this section of the book is about "Preparing Experienced Leaders to Finish Well," we will now focus on what John the Baptist did as the experienced leader preparing the way for Jesus, the emerging leader.

If experienced leaders have the attitude of John the Baptist, then even if the succession plan does not go as hoped, the leadership transition and the emerging leader can still succeed. In the context of Jesus's emerging leadership and swelling crowds, here's what John said to all of his disciples, followers, and fans: "I must decrease" (John 3:30). That phrase was a confession of intent, a heart attitude, a prayer, and a promise. Wise and humble experienced leaders make that same confession, have that same heart attitude, pray that same prayer, and make that same promise. "I must decrease." (Not "I might decrease, if everything goes as planned.")

If we read a few verses before John's brilliant "I must decrease" confession, we will see four prerequisite confessions and attitudes that are foundational if the heart of an experienced leader is to embrace decrease.

Confession #1: "I am not the Christ" *(John 3:28).*

As long as a spiritual leader has a messianic complex, he or she will never voluntarily decrease in order to land the ministry plane or allow an emerging leader in the cockpit. The fact that John the Baptist promised to decrease is notable in light of what Jesus said about him: "Among those born of women there has arisen no one greater than John the Baptist" (Matthew 11:11). Most I-am-the-greatest type of leaders tend to develop a messianic complex and find no reason to ever decrease. Perhaps John's "I am not the Christ" confession was necessary to keep the messianic complex at bay. I know this was addressed in Chapter 1, but it is so important that I probably should have repeated it in every chapter. Again, my suggestion for pastors and ministry leaders, especially those with fame and crowds, is to daily look at yourself in the mirror, and repeat John's confession: "I am not the Christ." This will help you decrease when it is time to decrease.

Eugene Peterson warned pastors about the destructive seduction of crowds in his classic memoir, *The Pastor*. "There are three ways in which humans try to find transcendence—religious meaning—apart from God as revealed through the cross of Jesus: through the ecstasy of alcohol and drugs, through the ecstasy of recreational sex, ***through the ecstasy of crowds***. Church leaders frequently warn against the drugs and the sex, but at least, in America, almost never against the crowds."

The daily reminder: "I am not the Christ" is an effective antidote to the addictive "ecstasy of crowds."

Confession #2: "I have been sent before him" (*John 3:28*).

In order to decrease, it is vital to know who we are not, but also to know that we have been sent on mission by a higher authority. "Sentness" implies purpose and submission. The last two words in this confession—"before him"—imply that I am not the beginning and the end, the center and the focal point, that there is something (and someone) greater after me, thus the need for a leadership transition. Here's my second suggested daily confession for experienced leaders: "I am not the Christ, but I have been sent on a Christ-honoring mission."

Confession #3: "He must increase" (*John 3:30*).

He, in this case, is Jesus. John, the experienced leader, acknowledged the inevitable rise of Jesus. He **must** increase. This acknowledgment left no room for shifting emotions or changing plans. John committed himself to the process of seeing Jesus take his place. There would be no ifs, ands, or buts. This commitment provided stability during a time of change. Both the experienced leader and the emerging leader knew what to expect. Because of John's commitment to Jesus, neither was blindsided with unexpected changes. John landed his plane.

Confession #4: "I must decrease" *(John 3:30).*

Likewise, John accepted the imperative—I **must** decrease. We always must decrease so Jesus can increase. From a leadership runway perspective, John was decreasing speed in order to land, as Jesus was increasing speed to take off. To avoid runway crashes, the experienced leader must always decrease as the emerging leader increases.

If the greatest living human (named John the Baptist in Matthew 11:7-11) could confess, "I am not the Christ, I have been sent, he must increase, I must decrease," then we who are less than the greatest living human can certainly make the same four-fold confession and embrace the decrease attitude.

Here's a question to ponder as you consider the inevitability of your ministry decrease: Are you okay if the next generation forgets your contribution, if they leave you out of the story, or if you do not get the credit you think you deserve?

FORGOTTEN OLD DONKEYS

The story of the Triumphal Entry contains a painful metaphor for experienced leaders who have decreased so emerging leaders can increase. All four Gospels include the story, with slight but significant nuances.

John's account is the simplest: "Jesus found a young donkey and sat on it" (John 12:14).

Luke tells us a bit more about that donkey: "Find a colt tied, on which no one has ever yet sat" (Luke 19:30). What John described as a "young donkey," Luke called a colt. Same thing. Luke informs us that the young colt is tied up, has never carried weight, and that "the Lord has need of it" (Luke 19:31). Shocking note to experienced donkeys who have carried much ministry weight for many years: "the Lord has need of" young inexperienced donkeys who have never carried weight.

Every emerging leader wants to do the work of the ministry, but few want to carry the weight of ministry. Most emerging leaders are tied up and need a leader with experience to untie them. The leadership runway is the place for experienced leaders to untie emerging leaders so that emerging leaders can start carrying greater leadership weight.

Since Mark's Gospel was probably Luke's main source, their accounts are almost identical. The main difference is Mark's multiple use of his favorite word, "immediately" (Mark 11:1-4). Mark communicates an urgency in finding and untying the young donkey. In the context of leadership transition, I hope you feel an urgency in discovering and "untying" emerging next generation leaders.

In Matthew's version of the story, Jesus sent two disciples to a village with clear instructions: "Find a donkey tied, **and** a colt with her." Jesus then said to "untie **them** and bring **them** to me." He also instructed the two disciples how to explain why they untied the donkeys: "The Lord needs **them**" (Matthew 21:2-3). Did you notice that Matthew added a character to the story that Mark, Luke, and John completely left out?

All four gospel writers mention a young donkey that has never carried weight ("never sat on"). Only Matthew mentions that there were two donkeys in the story—an old donkey and a young donkey- and that "the Lord needs **them**" not just one or the other.

As experienced leaders (old donkeys) decrease and emerging leaders (young donkeys) increase, the spotlight will increasingly shine on the new leaders and off the older leaders. Some experienced leaders handle that transition well. Many do not. Mark, Luke, and John only mentioned the young donkey, completely ignoring the old donkey—the donkey that has carried weight, the donkey that has taken care of the young colt, the donkey that is decreasing but deserving of recognition.

What if you are left out of the narrative? Part of what it means to decrease so the next generation can increase is accepting that the spotlight will increasingly be on the new leaders and off the old leaders. The sooner old donkeys embrace this fact, the better the transition will be.

If Jesus chooses to use the young generation and chooses to leave the old donkeys out of the story when it's told, I hope and pray that my generation will not respond like one of the insecure donkeys (for example, King Saul) in the Old Testament.

THE DELUSION OF CELEBRITY

Here's a sad but common story. David has killed Goliath, and on the way home, "the women came out of all the cities of Israel, singing and dancing, to meet King Saul, with tambourines, with songs of joy, and with musical instruments. And the women sang to one another as they celebrated, 'Saul has struck down his thousands, and David his ten thousands'" (1 Samuel 18:6-7).

David was experiencing a little bit of fame and celebrity. Perhaps he was unaware that fans always exaggerate the facts. The song claimed that David struck down "ten thousands" when he actually struck down one—a big one, but still only one. Adoring social media fans can add one plus zero and come up with "ten thousands."

These same singing female fans gave Saul credit for "thousands" which was also an exaggeration. Fans and followers, whether real or digital, always exaggerate. The problem is when leaders foolishly embrace celebrity and actually believe inflated reports about their own public greatness. Celebrity is dangerous to the Christian soul. Fame and celebrity distort reality, deform the soul, and corrupt godly character. Spiritual leaders should run from celebrity, not run to it.

When the next generation starts getting more credit than our generation, I hope we won't react like Saul who was so insecure that he tried to kill David. Too many experienced but insecure leaders metaphorically kill potential next-generation leaders.

None of this is unique to Saul and David. It still happens today, but there is a better way.

It does not matter what you are leading, how long you have been leading, or whether you did a great job or utterly failed. At some point you will vacate your leadership position, and another will fill it and carry the leadership weight. Since every leadership position is temporary, there will always be another leadership transition. Hopefully, the leadership transition will be based on a written succession plan. Designing a wise succession plan starts with the acknowledgment that no one leads forever. Leaders who refuse to talk about their own mortality are the same people who typically fail to write wills and succession plans.

The King Saul to Shepherd David leadership transition was exactly how not to do succession. Remember, Saul attempted to kill David on several occasions. Did David learn from Saul's mistakes? It seems he did. Let's jump ahead to the end of David's life. As he faces his own mortality, King David is working diligently to ensure as smooth a leadership transition as possible. Perhaps David was thinking about how he wished Saul had treated him as a successor. Here's the preamble to David's succession plan in his own words: "Solomon, my son is **young and inexperienced**, and the house that has to be built for the Lord **must be exceedingly magnificent** of fame and glory throughout all lands. I will therefore make preparations." Watch what David did after acknowledging the reality of his son's inexperience: "So David provided material in great quantity before his death" (1 Chronicles 22:5).

Solomon is like that young colt that has never been ridden—never carried heavy weight, never accomplished much of anything. The calling, the purpose, the plan of God is magnificent. It's huge. When the leadership weight is obviously beyond the capacity of young next-generation leaders, too many experienced leaders retract their landing gear and head back to the comfort of cruising altitude, leaving the leadership runway and their successors behind.

Realizing that the mission is beyond the capacity of the successor makes it tempting to abort the landing. That's rarely a good idea, especially on a Facebook Live broadcast. Better to follow David's example. The Scripture quoted above tells us that David did two things to help the next generation succeed: preparation and provision. He made preparations for the work of building the magnificent temple and he provided great quantities of necessary resources. Wise preparation and abundant provision go a long way to help a young inexperienced leader succeed in an overwhelmingly demanding new role.

THE LEADERSHIP RUNWAY 

At some point, no matter how clearly we are called and no matter how successful we have been, every leader will have to land the leadership plane so a new leader can occupy the cockpit and taxi down the runway to take off.

One of the most important jobs of every leader is succession planning. *The Leadership Runway* includes a three-part succession planning strategy: 1) preparing emerging leaders to lead the organization, 2) preparing the organization to be led by emerging leaders, and 3) preparing experienced leaders to finish well.

Final words of wisdom for experienced leaders as you prepare to land on the leadership runway:

- You must decrease so that Jesus can increase. Decrease is part of the Christian life, for the rest of your life.
- You must decrease so that your successor can increase. Decreasing so Jesus can increase is a no-brainer for Christian leaders. Decreasing so your successor can increase is a bit more difficult, but still necessary.

- You are not the Messiah, no matter how often adoring crowds, fans, and social media followers offer messianic devotion.
- You are still called, so stay on mission!
- When you feel like a forgotten and unappreciated old donkey, get over it.

You might be left out of future iterations of the story, but at least the story is still being told.

CHAPTER 13

Set Your House in Order

Hello. My name is Inigo Montoya. You killed my father. Prepare to die.

—Inigo Montoya

Set your house in order, for you shall die.

—Prophet Isaiah, 2 Kings 20:1

The tragic story of King Hezekiah is one of many biblical reminders of the temporary nature of life, the urgent need for succession planning, and the unavoidable reality of leadership transition.

About 680 years before the birth of Jesus, Hezekiah was sick and "at the point of death." God sent the prophet Isaiah with a succession planning message: "Set your house in order, for you shall die." The king responded with a desperate prayer of faith. God sent his prophet back with an updated message: "I have heard your prayer … I will add fifteen years to your life" (2 Kings 20:1-6). God's gracious gift of 15 bonus years did not eliminate Hezekiah's impending leadership transition or the urgency of succession planning. The king would still die and another king would assume his leadership position. The 15 years simply gave him extra time to set his house in order.

Whether you have 15 extra years or a fast approaching date with retirement or death, this "set your house in order" word applies to every experienced leader. For outgoing leaders to finish well, they must prepare the ministry and the upcoming leaders for the future. That's what it means to set your ministry house in order. But there's more. The outgoing leader must also prepare himself, his heart, his finances, and his family for the future. That's what it means to set your own house in order.

PREPARING TO FINISH WELL

As previously mentioned, my doctoral research revealed seven major findings that emerged in the context of my official dissertation problem and purpose statement, which was "to discover why some denominations, mission organizations, and megachurches achieve post-founder-generation sustainability while others do not and to determine next steps for succession planning and leadership transition in Every Nation Churches & Ministries."

My seven major findings—seven preparation points—can be divided into two distinct categories: 1) setting your ministry house in order, and 2) setting your personal house in order. We have already examined the first two of the seven preparation points in Parts II and III. Points three through seven address areas of personal preparation for the experienced leader as the time to land approaches.

I feel it is important as experienced leaders prepare to land on the leadership runway, to present these seven preparation points together as a whole. All seven are necessary for the experienced leader to finish well. None can be ignored.

So, ladies and gentlemen, as we prepare to land, please remain seated with your seatbelts fastened until the captain turns off the Fasten Seat Belt sign. Please use caution when opening the overhead bins, so your carry-on junk does not conk you on the head. And before deplaning, make sure you have given your best shot at accomplishing these seven steps to ensure that you finish well.

1. Prepare Emerging Leaders to Lead the Ministry

Long before my dissertation research, I instinctively knew that post-founder sustainability would depend, at least in part, on successfully preparing new leaders to lead the organizations that I currently led. The local church, global mission organization, and extension ministries I have led for multiple decades, have all had a strong emphasis on leadership development and multi-generational leadership empowerment. If our ministries are to thrive beyond current leadership, then experienced leaders must identify potential leaders, develop future leaders, and empower emerging leaders. We discover and develop new leaders when we look for and focus on sanctified hearts, skilled hands, spiritual habits, and sacred callings.

As experienced leaders, once you have identified, developed, and empowered emerging leaders to take your place, is that all that is necessary? Not quite. As leaders discuss succession and transition, a good starting point is to acknowledge that leadership transition is more of a continual process than a one-and-done event. Most succession planning focuses on a leadership baton exchange between an established leader and an emerging leader. However, unless the established leader is the founder of the organization, he or she will actually experience at least two leadership transitions. In the first transition, the leadership baton is received. In the second transition, the baton is passed to the next generation. In the first transition, you are the increasing leader. In the second transition you are the decreasing leader.

Jesus experienced leadership transitions from both perspectives. As John the Baptist decreased, he passed his leadership influence to Jesus, who was increasing. That was the first, but not the last, leadership transition for Jesus. Selecting his original 12 disciples was the starting point of his own succession plan that eventually led to him passing the mission to his disciples.

Once a leadership team accepts this continual process principle, that means that succession planning and leadership transition is an ongoing conversation as long as the ministry is living. I don't mean that it is discussed daily. That wouldn't be smart. But it should be revisited at least annually—more often if the experienced leader is really really old, in poor health, forgetting everybody's name, or playing golf most of the time.

2. Prepare the Ministry to Be Led by Emerging Leaders

Until my dissertation research, it had not dawned on me that ministry organizations would need to be prepared in order to be led by emerging leaders. In *To Change the World*, James Hunter makes the case that as important as individuals are to the mission of God, individuals are nevertheless inadequate. The organizations and institutions that individuals develop are also essential to the mission. "The passion to engage the world, to shape it and finally to change it for the better" requires "individual and corporate, public and private" engagement.[1] In the leadership classic, *Spiritual Leadership*, J. Oswald Sanders wrote, "The true test of a person's leadership is the health of the organization when the organizer is gone."[2] Once their founders are no longer leading, some churches and ministries grow stronger and larger, while too many grow weaker and smaller. In order to prepare a ministry organization to stay on mission as it is led by emerging leaders, the outgoing leaders must work on three aspects of the organization: cultivating healthy culture, creating simple systems, and constructing flexible structures.

3. Prepare Experienced Leaders to Finish Well

In order to prepare for their future, experienced leaders must reevaluate their attitudes toward succession, reimagine life after their current positions, and review their finances. As stated earlier, many pastors and ministry leaders have given little thought to retirement or succession planning, with almost 30% saying they will never retire. This explains the gap between the average age of senior leader retirement in the corporate world and those in the ministry world.* The unavoidable reality is that when experienced leaders are unprepared for life after the ministry version of the C-suite, they tend to hold on to their current positions too long. While it is ultimately the responsibility of experienced leaders to prepare themselves to finish well, a functional eldership, a wise legal board, and a mature oversight team should work with outgoing leaders in all aspects of preparation.[3]

4. Prepare the Heart

My research taught me that ministry succession from founders to second-generation leaders is the most difficult, often because

---

*A major reason for holding on too long will be addressed in Point 5: Prepare the Finances.

the founders did not prepare their hearts to let go emotionally. My observation and experience taught me that founders and long-tenured leaders have a difficult time letting go and moving on. More than their successors, founders tend to have their identities enmeshed with their ministries. A founder's organizational identity, unclear future, and messianic complex combine to create the perfect emotional storm that can sink the best succession plan. Thus, the importance of heart preparation. When Paul wrote to Timothy and Titus about qualifications for church leadership, his lists were heavy on relational character qualities with no mention of academic credentials or organizational management skills. For Paul, preparing leaders was preparing the heart. Since God promises to resist the proud and give grace to the humble, character development, especially the character quality of humility, is vital for experienced leaders and emerging leaders to succeed during and after transition.

5. Prepare the Finances

Too many pastors and ministry leaders have not made wise financial preparation and therefore hold on to ministry positions longer than they should, to the detriment of the individual and the organization. Others do not hold on, but they move on to financially insecure futures. Both situations can be avoided if we make financial preparation part of succession planning. Wise and generous financial preparation will benefit emerging leaders, experienced leaders, and the organization.

While most top corporate executives retire with plenty of money, it is the opposite for most pastors and ministry leaders. This lack of adequate financial preparation tempts many spiritual leaders to hold on to their positions and salaries far too long. Many ministry leaders simply cannot afford to retire, so they don't.

A starting point for financial preparation is for a leader to adopt a reasonable theology of money at the beginning of the job rather than just before retirement. A biblical view of money includes hard work, disciplined saving, wise investing, as well as frugality, contentment, faith, and generosity. These biblical principles, if applied early in a career, will make it much less likely that a leader will hold on to a position just for the salary.

6. Prepare Relationships, Especially Spouses

Corporate CEOs tend to socialize with other CEOs, rather than with people from their office. Not so in the church and mission world, where pastors and leaders not only have their identity tied to their jobs, but their friends tend to be their ministry colleagues. When the CEO retires, their social circles are not necessarily disrupted. However, a ministry position change almost always means social and relational disruption. Without question, the most important relationship affected by leadership transition is the spouse. Six times in the past three decades, Deborah and I have transitioned the senior leadership of a church or ministry from us to another leader. Because we did leadership, succession, and transition together, we experienced little relational pain when emerging leaders replaced us. I have observed multiple leadership transitions where the spouse of the experienced leader was either ignorant of—or not in agreement with—the succession plan. That's a formula for disaster. The leader's spouse is the most important and most neglected person in many ministry succession plans. Biblical wisdom and basic honor demands that we include the spouse at pertinent intervals throughout the succession process. There are many relationships impacted by ministry succession, none as important as the spouse.

7. Prepare to Adjust Your Timetable

A successful leadership transition is not dependent on following the exact timetable specified by the succession plan. I have observed ministry leadership transitions that went exactly according to the plan, and others that were not even close. I interviewed a former megachurch leader who indicated that the succession plan time-table was suddenly cut in half by his successor. A mission founder reported that he had to speed up his unwritten succession plan because of a ministry emergency in another nation. Despite not adhering to the original timetable, both of these ministries con-tinue to thrive. In *The Elephant in the Boardroom*, Carolyn Weese addresses the timing of succession planning and leadership tran-sition: "Because every pastor is a departing pastor, the day to begin thinking about a transition plan is the day the pastor arrives."[4] Rather than taking Weese's advice, many leaders wait as long as possible to think about their transition. Vanderbloemen's book opens with this sentence: "Every pastor is an interim pastor."[5] This reality is the reason for *The Leadership Runway* book. While I encourage experienced leaders and their teams to talk about min-istry succession sooner rather than later, leadership transition can be successful even if that wisdom is rejected and the process is delayed, or if the timetable needs adjustment midstream.

THE LEADERSHIP RUNWAY 

Because no one lives or leads forever, there will be a leadership transition. And another. And another. Ad infinitum. Wise leaders recognize the temporary nature of their leadership positions and set their ministry house in order by preparing emerging leaders to lead the ministry and preparing the ministry to be led by emerging leaders. They set their own houses in order by preparing them-selves to finish well. Wise self preparation includes financial, voca-tional, relational, emotional, and especially spousal preparation.

Afterword

You can't let your failures define you. You have to let your failures teach you.

–Barack Obama

I have no greater joy than to hear that my children are walking in the truth.

–Apostle John, 3 John 1:4

While my first leadership transition was a colossal failure (Chapter 2: "Admitting My Greatest Leadership Failure"), I did learn from it. After the miracle on Herbert Street turned into the mosque on Herbert Street, I was determined, by the grace of God, to never have another succession fail. In ministry, too much is at stake to fail at leadership transition again.*

My next four leadership transitions succeeded.** None were done the same way, but they all worked out in the end. Some were abrupt, others were gradual. Some were announced with precise

---

*Transition failures result from not only individual failures, but also organizational and structural failures. Sometimes, the resulting failure is beyond the control of any individual. At the end of the day, any time a church dissolves and is then turned into a mosque, or a bookstore, or a bed and breakfast, a failure of some kind has occurred. The goal of every leader should be to ensure that the vision and life of the organization they're leaving is healthy and vibrant, ready for the next leader.

**See Preface.

communication plans, others were never announced, we just let them happen and assumed people would eventually notice that I was gone. They were all different, mainly because I had no clue what I was doing. Often I was making it up in the moment, improvising in real time. In those days, I never had a written succession plan, but the leadership transitions worked anyway. I was doing something right, but until my Asbury dissertation research, I couldn't explain why my successors were succeeding. Now I know that our healthy church and ministry culture contributed, and my insistence on homegrown leaders rather than imports flattened the learning curve for our emerging leaders. But I'm sure our leadership transition successes were primarily due to common grace.

This book ends where it started, with two quotes from the first chapter. Jacko Willink, retired US Navy SEAL, now author and business consultant, constantly talks and writes about "extreme ownership" which simply means to take complete ownership of whatever happens on your watch. In his words, "Leaders must own everything in their world. There is no one else to blame."[1] After describing a life-and-death situation that did not go according to the plan, Willink wrote, "I had to take complete ownership of what went wrong. That is what a leader does—even if it means getting fired. If anyone was to be blamed and fired for what happened, let it be me."[2]

Willink continues, "There are no bad teams, only bad leaders."[3] He defines bad leaders as those who pass the blame to others rather than taking extreme ownership. When it comes to succession planning and leadership transition, it is easy and common to blame failure on the leader who receives the leadership baton. I agree with the Willink doctrine that if things don't work out, ultimately it is the responsibility of the experienced leader whose job was not only to lead, but also to create a reasonable succession plan and execute a healthy leadership transition.

The other quote that started this book was from the Apostle Paul, who wrote the following to the church in Corinth: "The fire will test what sort of work each one has done. If the work that anyone has built on the foundation survives, he will receive a reward. If anyone's work is burned up, he will suffer loss, though he himself will be saved, but only as through fire" (1 Corinthians 3:13-15).

Knowing that our work will be tested by fire, leaders have no choice but to learn how to craft a succession plan and how to execute a leadership transition. The goal of *The Leadership Runway* is to help you fireproof your life work, so that after you are no longer leading, the ministry is still thriving.

I pray that you will never see your version of the Miracle on Herbert Street turn into a Mosque on Herbert Street. By God's grace, I trust that whatever you are called to lead will outlive you and will grow stronger, larger, and more influential when the next generation is leading.

The Lasting Power of Christian Institutions

Like John Wesley and Aimee Semple McPherson, Billy Graham and Ignatius of Loyola not only did great ministry work while they were alive, but also built institutions that continue their mission to this day.

BILLY GRAHAM (1918-2018)

Billy Graham was an evangelist, perhaps the most productive and prolific evangelist in history. During his lifetime he conducted 417 evangelistic mass crusades (later called "missions") in 185 nations. An estimated 215 million people heard him preach at these live events, with another 2.2 billion people hearing him preach via television and radio. More than 3 million people responded to Graham's altar calls to "accept Jesus as personal savior." As impressive as those numbers are, because Graham built Christian institutions, every statistical category that matters to an evangelist will certainly be surpassed in time.

Here is a partial list of institutions founded or cofounded by Billy Graham.

- Billy Graham Evangelistic Association (BGEA). Established in 1950, BGEA continues to conduct evangelistic missions (formerly called "crusades") around the world, featuring the preaching of Graham's children and grandchildren.
- Worldwide Pictures (WWP). Established in 1951, WWP has produced and distributed over 125 evangelistic films.
- Christianity Today (CT) magazine. Established in 1956, CT has over 2.5 million monthly readers.
- Gordon Conwell Theological Seminary (GCTS). Co-founded by Graham in 1969, GCTS has over 10,000 alumni all over the world, and continues to train pastors, preachers, and vocational ministers.
- Evangelical Council for Financial Accountability (ECFA). In 1979, in the midst of great Evangelical growth and several infamous ministry financial scandals, ECFA was formed by BGEA along with World Vision and other ministries, to create financial standards and accountability for the management of ministry finance. Today there are over 2100 ECFA member organizations, including Every Nation Churches & Ministries.

Though Graham passed away in 2018 (when he was 99!), his influence continues through the BGEA, Worldwide Pictures, CT magazine, Gordon Conwell, and ECFA.

IGNATIUS OF LOYOLA (1491–1556)

In 1540, 10 men with no money and no experience, but with big vision, set out to change the world. They instinctively knew that their task would require them to develop leaders, so they focused on developing leaders and doing it quickly. Within a decade, despite their lack of experience in higher education, they had established over 30 colleges in Europe. By the end of the 1700s, they had over 700 schools on 5 continents. Today the Jesuits are the world's largest religious order, including over 2000 institutions,* in over 100 nations, run by an army of over 21,000 highly committed lifers, including Pope Francis.[1]

I don't agree with every point of their theology or mission strategy, but after decades of experience working with graduates of Jesuit educational institutions in the Philippines, I can say that they are still doing an excellent job of developing leaders. I've hired and worked with graduates from public schools, secular private schools, Evangelical schools, and Catholic schools, but the Jesuit institutions in the Philippines seem to crank out a higher ratio of leaders than their educational competitors.

---

*I'm not sure why, but it seems like the most well-known Jesuit institutions in the USA are equally known for their high academic standards and their basketball teams—Georgetown, Marquette, Gonzaga, Loyola Marymount, Creighton.

When Legal Boards Are Required

Best Practices

1. Discussion: ends, not means
2. Focus: mission, not methods
3. Goal: define and delegate, not react and ratify
4. Decisions: rigorous debate, not rubber stamp
5. Communication: speak as one voice, not as individuals

Worst Practices

1. Mission Drift: discuss anything and everything
2. Micromanage Executives: insufficient delegation of authority
3. Mismanage Budget: too few or too many executive limits
4. Membership in Perpetuity: no terms, no term limits
5. Monitoring Inconsistencies: no consistent executive accountability

Board Meeting Template

1. Call to order
2. Devotional word and prayer (5-10 mins)

3. Review organizational mission, values, board responsibilities, and best practices (5-10 min)
4. Review and approve previous board minutes (5-10 mins)
5. Business matters
   a. Budget
   b. Executive director report and ministry update (based on job description)
   c. Succession planning update
   d. Other matters
6. Schedule next board meeting
7. Close in prayer

Leadership Transitions and Spiritual Warfare

To do ministry succession and leadership transition wisely, experienced and emerging leaders must consider organizational, spiritual, and relational perspectives. A common mistake is to focus primarily on the organizational and relational, while ignoring or underestimating spiritual realities.

The Bible writers present dozens of succession planning and leadership transition accounts. Some are exemplary, filled with timeless leadership lessons that are easily applicable today. Most are cautionary tales about the spiritual side of succession including pride, greed, folly, idolatry, immorality, unforgiveness, and invisible demonic entities. When leadership transitions go wrong, the autopsy usually reveals a combination of human sin, relational dysfunction, and evil spiritual forces.

I am not one to obsess over devils, demons, dark angels, and satanic strongholds, but a serious reading of Scripture forces me to acknowledge that there are invisible evil forces working overtime, especially during leadership transitions. In story after story we find that the most challenging circumstances happened during generational leadership transfer. Some of those transition diffi-culties are, at least in part, due to what Paul calls "spiritual forces of evil in the heavenly places" (Ephesians 6:12). Peter warns the church leaders in Asia Minor to be "sober-minded" and "watchful" because "your adversary the devil prowls around like a roaring lion, seeking someone to devour" (1 Peter 5:8).

In the Bible's succession stories, sometimes the influence of "the devil" and his "spiritual forces of evil" are explicit, other times assumed, but always "seeking someone to devour." I am tired of seeing people devoured because of unwise or nonexistent suc-cession plans.

Each of the following leadership transitions failed either rela-tionally, organizationally, or spiritually. Some achieved the failure trifecta, botching all three. No matter how we describe the surface problem in most succession fails, if we dig deep enough we will always discover spiritual roots, for better or for worse. Notice the negative spiritual influence* in the following succession stories.

Joshua to the Next Generation

The Moses to Joshua transition was relatively smooth, compared to others, but the Joshua to the following generation transition was a disaster. What happened? Joshua and his leadership team did a great job leading but failed at succession planning and leadership transition. "The people served the Lord all the days of Joshua, and all the days of the elders who outlived Joshua." That's good, but inadequate. After Joshua died, "there arose another generation after them who did not know the Lord or the work that he had done for Israel." That's not good. It is the job of experienced leaders, not only to lead well, but also to identify, equip, and empower next genera-tion leaders. On an organizational level, this succession failure can be attributed to Joshua's weak leadership pipeline, however when

---

*"Negative spiritual influence" is a less Charismatic/Pentecostal way to say spiritual warfare, demonic attack, and war in the heavenlies.

a whole generation of potential leaders "did not know the Lord," that points to an underlying spiritual problem. (See Judges 2:7-13.) Perhaps if better spiritual habits had been established, this generational fail could have been avoided. Maybe a revival or two would have done the trick. No matter the theoretical solution, the real problem was primarily spiritual, not organizational or relational.

King Saul to David

Saul always assumed his son Jonathan would be his successor. When it became obvious that David was the man, Saul attempted to murder him on multiple occasions. David did nothing to deserve Saul's murderous wrath. After all, he killed Saul's giant enemy, married Saul's daughter, and befriended Saul's son. Plus, he risked his life to lead Saul's army and even performed private harp concerts to soothe the king when he experienced fits of anxiety and depression. If David so loyally and sacrificially served his king, why did Saul try to kill him? Like all ministry successions and leadership transitions, there was an invisible and insidious spiritual side to the story. Prophet Samuel describes the unseen spiritual entity as a "harmful spirit" that came on Saul while David was playing live worship music. Under the influence of that invisible "harmful spirit," Saul threw a battle spear, hoping to "pin David to the wall" (1 Samuel 18:10-11). Again, we see a demonic entity inserting itself into the succession story. Hopefully, when we are the experienced leader facing our successor, we will do better than Saul, and when we are the emerging leader, we will be as honorable as David.

Old Testament to New Testament

The birth, life, death, and resurrection of Jesus marked the transition from old covenant to new covenant. As soon as Jesus was born in a Bethlehem barn, King Herod pretended to be a worshiper, but he was actually a murderer. His secret goal was to kill the real King of the Jews. Herod was willing to murder multiple innocent babies just in case one of them happened to be his potential successor. That's a seriously violent "harmful spirit" at work right there!

Carpenter to Preacher

About three decades later, Jesus was experiencing his ministry transition from local carpenter to itinerant preacher. This transition included intense spiritual preparation: 40 days of prayer and fasting in the wilderness. During this preparation time, Jesus experienced demonic attacks and tricky Scripture-twisting temptations. But that's not all. As they did at his birth scene, angels also started showing up during his wilderness preparation and temptation. Whether we acknowledge their presence or not, ministry transitions often involve the invisible world of angels and demons.

Jesus to the Disciples

Three years later, as Jesus was preparing to transition the global mission of God to his original disciples, he experienced the agony of Gethsemane, the pain of betrayal, false accusations, unjust arrest, violent torture, and execution on a cross. While the list in the previous sentence includes relational conflicts that cause painful human emotion, it also includes satanic attacks. Luke explained it bluntly: "Then Satan entered into Judas. He went away and conferred with the chief priests and officers how he might betray him (Jesus)" (Luke 22:3-4). There are two leadership transition lessons in these two verses. First, Judas's betrayal was more than a natural human relational conflict, it was satanic. Second, Satan attacks important relationships during leadership transitions.

VICTORY THROUGH JESUS!

This brief survey of leadership succession and transition in the Bible reveals that Satan and his demons are aggressively active during takeoff and landing—when experienced leaders are decreasing so that emerging leaders can increase, when experienced leaders are handing the baton to emerging leaders, when experienced leaders are landing and emerging leaders are about to take off. Transition time is when leaders and ministries are most vulnerable. That's when Satan throws the kitchen sink at experienced and emerging leaders.

These Bible stories also reveal that succession and transition is when the Holy Spirit and his angels seem to be most active.

Here's the take away for ministry leaders: while you are doing the organizational and relational work to ensure the best succession and transition possible, don't neglect the spiritual aspect. Expect Satan to attack relationships, but be confident that it is "God, who gives us the victory through our Lord Jesus Christ" (1 Corinthians 15:57)!

Acknowledgments

The journey that resulted in this book, started in 2013 during a spiritual retreat with five close friends and ministry colleagues. After a morning of prayer and reflection, we discussed what it might look like to finish well. For me, finishing well meant replacing myself in the global ministry organization I helped start. I had no idea how or when to do that.

Two years later, Asbury Theological Seminary representatives contacted me to discuss the possibility of partnering with Every Nation for graduate level leadership development. Sensing a providential moment, I promptly enrolled in Asbury's Doctor of Ministry program. The next week I recruited seven Every Nation leaders to take the journey with me, in the hope that peer pressure would keep me from dropping out of seminary, yet again.

For the next three years, I woke up and went to bed thinking about "Post-Founder Sustainability: Building Ministries that Outlive Their Founders." During my Asbury experience I not only learned what I needed to learn, I also adopted new and better ways to learn. For that, I owe a debt of gratitude to some Asbury people:

- With profound gratitude to the team that drove from Wilmore to Nashville to explain how Asbury could serve Every Nation: Dr. Milton Lowe, Dr. Gregg Okesson, and Dr. Tom Tumblin. This book would not exist if you had not taken that road trip to Nashville.

- With heartfelt thanks to my dissertation coach who introduced me to authors I would have never discovered on my own and who constantly challenged me to think beyond the obvious: Dr. Russell West. You influenced this book (and Every Nation's future) more than you'll ever know.
- With a thankful shout-out to my Asbury classmates: Dr. Manny Carlos, Dr. David Houston, Dr. Chris Johnson, Dr. Noel Landicho, Dr. Nixon Ng, Dr. Delvin Pikes, and Dr. Brian Taylor. "We from Asbury, bro!"
- With special thanks to Dr. Ellen Marmon for leading the Asbury DMin program with grace, wisdom, and strength, and for welcoming the "Asbury 8" with open arms.

I also owe a lifelong debt of gratitude to those five men who were part of that 2013 spiritual retreat: Russ Austin, Phil Bonasso, Brett Fuller, Jim Laffoon, and Kevin York.* It is a privilege doing life and ministry with you men. Thanks for serving as a wise and honest sounding board for every concept in this book.

I owe an eternal debt of gratitude to all the Victory Church Manila leaders, especially my direct successors. Your faithfulness makes me look like a better leader than I am. It is an illustrious honor to serve on the Victory Bishops' Council with six of the finest men I know: Manny Carlos, Ferdie Cabiling, Gilbert Foliente, Jun Escosar, Juray Mora, and Michael Paderes.

Transforming an academic dissertation into a useful book proved to be much more frustrating and time consuming than I expected. I could not have done it without the help of brutally honest editors, detailed fact checkers, brilliant research assistants, and big-picture ideators. I'm talking about you—Carlos Antonio, Varsha Daswani, Laura Lloyd, Karen Montgomery, Rachel Murrell, William Murrell**, and Keziah Tabelisma.

---

* "The Five Guys"

** "Dad, this paragraph sounds like 'Dissertation Steve' again. Delete it, start over, and write something useful and readable for Every Nation global leaders."

Special thanks to graphic artist extraordinaire, Sam Barker, along with Kristen Oakley, for the cover design. Thanks also to world renowned aviation oracle, Barry Lee. Seriously, walking across the hall from the Every Nation global office to the Every Nation Seminary office to ask Barry about a little known runway fact, passenger jet crash data, or anything about flying, was much quicker than asking Siri or Google. Barry is a 6 foot 7 inch encyclopedia of aviation knowledge. Of course, I'd be remiss if I didn't thank Nolan Mueller* for his hard work marketing this book and getting it into your hands.

And finally, Deborah Murrell. It was fitting that we celebrated our 40th anniversary (in a Muslim nation) immediately after finishing the first draft of this book. Thank you for always being on this journey with me, no matter the place and no matter the cost. I can't imagine family, life (or global mission) without you. We are an amazing team!

---

*Nolan Mueller also controls all of my social media platforms. He decides what gets posted and what gets trashed, so all complaints should be sent directly to him, not to me.

ABOUT THE AUTHOR

In 1984, Steve and Deborah Murrell signed up for a one-month summer mission trip to Manila, Philippines, to help establish a church in Manila's University Belt. That one-month mission trip lasted a couple of decades.

That church, now known as Victory Church Manila, gathers for weekly worship in 18 Metro Manila locations, and empowers approximately 10,000 Victory Group leaders to make disciples in small groups. Victory has also established churches in over 150 Philippine cities and 22 nations.

In 1994, Rice Broocks and Phil Bonasso stopped in Manila on their way to explore ministry opportunities in Southeast Asia. That stop-over resulted in a global family of churches called Every Nation Churches & Ministries, which now works in over 80 nations.

In 2016 after 38 years in vocational ministry, Steve enrolled in Asbury Theological Seminary's Doctor of Ministry program. Three years of dissertation research eventually evolved into this book.

Along with serving as president of Every Nation, Steve is a preaching coach for Every Nation pastors around the world and a professor at Every Nation Seminary.* Every few years, he writes a book.

Steve and Deborah have three adult sons, three daughters-in-law, and nine grandchildren. They split their time between Nashville, Manila, and Delta Airlines.**

---

* Steve teaches Apostolic Leadership, Relational Discipleship, and Pastoral Theology at ENS.
** In his spare time, Steve can be seen on his Indian Chief Vintage cruising the hills and twisties of Middle Tennessee and beyond.

WikiChurch

Making Discipleship Engaging, Empowering, & Viral

100 Years from Now

Sustaining a Movement for Generations

My First, Second & Third Attempts at Parenting

Discovering the Heart of Parenting

Rediscovering Leadership

Identify, Develop, and Multiply Leaders

Previously published as *The Multiplication Challenge.*

The Purple Book

Biblical Foundations for Building Strong Disciples

End Notes

Introduction:

1. William Vanderbloemen and Warren Bird, *Next: Pastoral Succession That Works* (Baker Publishing Group, 2020), Kindle edition.

Chapter 2:

1. This tragic story came from the following five sources:

    a. Emma Green, "How Two Mississippi College Students Fell in Love and Decided to Join a Terrorist Group," *The Atlantic*, accessed 14 May 2023, https://www.theatlantic.com/politics/archive/2017/05/mississippi-young-dakhlalla/524751

    b. "Islamic Center of Mississippi, Inc., et al., Plaintiffs-appellants, v. City of Starkville, Mississippi, Defendant-appellee," Justia US Law, 1988, accessed 14 May 2023, https://law.justia.com/cases/federal/appellate-courts/F2/840/293/156666/

    c. Scott Bronstein and Drew Griffin, "Young ISIS Recruit: I was Blinded by Love," CNN, December 2016, accessed 14 May 2023, https://www.cnn.com/2016/12/02/us/mississippi-isis-muhammad-dakhlalla-interview/index.html

    d. "Muhammad Dakhlalla," Wikipedia, accessed 14 May 2023, https://en.wikipedia.org/wiki/Muhammad_Dakhlalla

    e. "Jaelyn Young," Wikipedia, accessed 14 May 2023, https://en.wikipedia.org/wiki/Jaelyn_Young

2. This part of the "Mosque on Herbert Street" story has been pulled from the following two sources.

   a. "Disbelief in Mississippi at How Far ISIS Message Can Travel," NY Times, 15 August 2025, accessed 14 April 2023, https://www.nytimes.com/2015/08/15/us/disbelief-in-mississippi-at-how-far-isis-message-can-travel.html

   b. "Mississippi Young Dakhlalla," *The Atlantic*, May 2017, accessed 14 April 2023. https://www.theatlantic.com/politics/archive/2017/05/mississippi-young-dakhlalla/524751/

Chapter 3

1. Steve Murrell, *100 Years From Now* (Dunham Books, 2013), Ch. 1.

2. John Pollock, *Wesley the Preacher* (Kingsway Publishing, 1989), 153.

3. J. C. Ryle, "A Sketch of the Life and Labors of George Whitefield," Monergism Library, accessed 14 April 2023. https://www.monergism.com/thethreshold/sdg/ryle/ryle_georgewhitefield.html

4. J. C. Ryle, "George Whitefield and His Ministry," Revival Library, accessed 13 April, 2023. https://www.revival-library.org/revival_heroes/18th_century/whitefield_george.shtml

5. Vinson Synan, *The Century of the Holy Spirit* (Thomas Nelson Publishers, 2001), iv.

6. Synan, *The Century of the Holy Spirit*, 257–258.

7. Makoto Fujimura, *Art and Faith: Theology of Making* (Yale University Press, 2021), 17.

8. Fujimura, *Art and Faith*, 18.

Part II

1. Thomas Merton, *No Man is an Island* (HarperOne, 2002), Kindle edition.

2. James K. A. Smith, *Desiring the Kingdom* (Baker Academic, 2009), Kindle edition.

Chapter 5

1. Malcolm Gladwell, *David and Goliath: Underdogs, Misfits, and the Art of Battling Giants*, 21, Kindle edition.

2. Gladwell, *David and Goliath*, 11, Kindle edition.

Chapter 6

1. M. Robert Mulholland, Jr., *Invitation to a Journey: A Road Map for Spiritual Formation* (IVP, Revised and Expanded edition, 2016), 898-899, Kindle edition.

2. Henri Nouwen, *Spiritual Formation: Following the Movements of the Spirit* (HarperOne, Reprint edition), Kindle edition.

3. Eugene Peterson, *Eat This Book: A Conversation in the Art of Spiritual Reading* (Eerdmans, 2009), Kindle edition.

4. Mulholland, *Invitation to a Journey*, 39, Kindle edition.

Chapter 7

1. Eugene Peterson, *Christ Plays in 10,000 Places* (Eerdmans, 2008), 77–79.

Chapter 8

1. Abby Ohlheiser, "Malcolm Gladwell's Cockpit Culture Theory and the Asiana Crash," *The Atlantic*, July 10, 2013, accessed 24 May 2023, https://www.theatlantic.com/national/archive/2013/07/malcolm-gladwells-cockpit-culture-theory-everywhere-after-asiana-crash/313442

2. William Vanderbloemen, *Culture Wins: The Roadmap to an Irresistible Workplace* (Savio Republic, 2020), 5, Kindle edition.

3. Maynard Webb, et al, *Dear Founder: Letters of Advice for Anyone Who Leads, Manages, or Wants to Start a Business* (St Martin's Press, 2018), 35.

4. Maynard, *Dear Founder*, 35.

5. Jim Collins, *Good to Great: Why Some Companies Make the Leap... and Others Don't* (Collins, 2001), Ch. 3: First Who ... Then What.

6. Vanderbloemen, *Culture Wins*, 55, Kindle edition.

7. Vanderbloemen, *Next: Pastoral Succession*, Kindle edition.

Chapter 9

1. Seth Stevenson, "The Southwest Secret: How the airline manages to turn a profit, year after year after year," Slate, June 12, 2012, accessed 14 April 2023. https://slate.com/business/2012/06/southwest-airlines-profitability-how-the-company-uses-operations-theory-to-fuel-its-success.html

2. Thom S. Rainer and Eric Geiger, *Simple Church* (B&H Books, 2011), ix.

3. Rainer & Geiger, *Simple Church*, 8.

4. Michael E. Gerber, *The E-Myth Revisited: Why Most Businesses Don't Work and What to Do About It* (HarperCollins e-books, 2009), Kindle edition.

5. Matthew Krimmel, "Why do Restaurants Fail? Restaurant Failure Rate, Statistics and Facts," BinWise, accessed 1 May 2023, https://home.binwise.com/blog/restaurant-failure-rate#:~:text=The%20National%20Restaurant%20Association%20estimates,within%205%20years%20of%20opening

6. "What is the Failure Rate for US Restaurants?," FoodIndustry.com, accessed 12 April 2023, https://www.foodindustry.com/articles/what-is-the-failure-rate-for-us-restaurants/

7. Gerber, *The E-Myth Revisited*, 85.

8. Gerber, *The E-Myth Revisited*, 238.

9. Gerber, *The E-Myth Revisited*, 234.

10. Chris Zook and James Allen, *The Founder's Mentality: How to Overcome the Predictable Crisis of Growth* (Harvard Business Review Press, 2016), 1.

11. Zook and Allen, *The Founder's Mentality*, 69-70.

12. Steve Murrell, *WikiChurch: Making Discipleship Engaging, Empowering, and Viral* (Charisma House, 2011).

13. Steve Murrell and William Murrell, *The Multiplication Challenge: A Strategy to Solve Your Leadership Shortage* (Creation House, 2016), 146-147.. Revised, updated, and republished in 2023 as *Rediscovering Leadership: Identify, Develop, and Multiply Leaders.*

14. Daniel A. Brown, *The Other Side of Pastoral Ministry* (Commended to The Word, 1996), 88.

15. Gerber, *The E-Myth Revisited.*

16. Fujimura, *Art + Faith*, 94.

Chapter 10

1. Craig S. Keener, *The IVP Bible Background Commentary: New Testament* (IVP Academic; 2nd edition, 2014), 134-135, Kindle edition.

2. Colin Marshall and Tony Payne, *The Trellis and the Vine* (Matthias Media; 2nd edition, 2021), 8.

3. Marshall & Payne, *The Trellis and the Vine*, 17.

4. Eddie L. Hyatt, *2000 Years of Charismatic Christianity* (Charisma House, 2002), 29.

5. Hyatt, *2000 Years of Charismatic Christianity*, 24.

6. Gerber, *The E-Myth Revisited*, 166-167, Kindle edition.

7. Gerber, *The E-Myth Revisited*, 166.

8. Peter F. Drucker, *Management: Tasks, Responsibilities, Practices* (Harper Collins, 1974), 628.

Chapter 11

1. Steve Murrell, "Post-Founder Sustainability: Building Ministries That Outlive Their Founders" (Doctor of Ministry thesis, Asbury Theological Seminary, 2019) pg. 127-128.

2. Vanderbloemen, *Next: Pastoral Succession That Works*, Kindle edition.

3. Os Guinness, *The Call: Finding and Fulfilling God's Purpose for Your Life* (Thomas Nelson, 2003).

Chapter 13

1. James Hunter, *To Change the World: The Irony, Tragedy, and Possibility of Christianity in the Late Modern World* (Oxford University Press, 2010).

2. J. Oswald Sanders, *Spiritual Leadership: Principles of Excellence for Every Believer* (Moody Publishers, 2017), Kindle edition.

3. For more information on possible changes to post-COVID-19 retirement ages, see the following article:
   Bob Woods, "From Disney to Target to Boeing, retirement is a thing of the past for CEO's." CNBC, Dec. 11, 2022; 10:00 AM EST, Updated Dec. 13, 2022; 4:49 PM EST, accessed 14 April, 2023. https://www.cnbc.com/2022/12/11/from-disney-to-target-boe-ing-ceo-retirements-are-a-thing-of-the-past.html

4. Carolyn Weese, *The Elephant in the Boardroom,* (Fortress Press, 2020), Ch. 3, Kindle edition.

5. Vanderbloemen, *Next: Pastoral Succession that Works*, 1.

Afterword

1. Jocko Willink, *Extreme Ownership: How U.S. Navy Seals Lead and Win* (St. Martin's Publishing Group, 2017), 14, Kindle edition.

2. Willink, *Extreme Ownership: How U.S. Navy Seals Lead and Win*, 26–27, Kindle edition.

3. Willink, *Extreme Ownership: How U.S. Navy Seals Lead and Win,* 49, Kindle edition.

Appendix A

1. Chris Lowney, *Heroic Leadership* (Loyola Press, 2003), 7.

Made in United States
Cleveland, OH
05 March 2025

14924746R00142